THREE WORKS
BY DYLAN THOMAS

ORIGINALLY PUBLISHED 1940-1952.

Three Works by Dylan Thomas
This book edition was created and published by Mamba Press
©MambaPress 2024

Contents

A Child's Christmas in Wales

    Portrait of the Artist as a Young Dog

        The Peaches
        A Visit to Grandpa's
        Patricia, Edith, and Arnold
        The Fight
        Extraordinary Little Cough
        Just Like Little Dogs
        Where Tawe Flows
        Who Do You Wish Was With Us?
        Old Garbo
        One Warm Saturday

    Under Milk Wood

A Child's Christmas in Wales

One Christmas was so much like the other, in those years around the sea-town corner now, out of all sound except the distant speaking of the voices I sometimes hear a moment before sleep, that I can never remember whether it snowed for six days and six nights when I was twelve, or whether it snowed for twelve days and twelve nights when I was six.

All the Christmases roll down towards the two-tongued sea, like a cold and headlong moon bundling down the sky that was our street; and they stop at the rim of the ice-edged, fish-freezing waves, and I plunge my hands in the snow and bring out whatever I can find. In goes my hand into that wool-white bell-tongued ball of holidays resting at the rim of the carol-singing sea, and out come Mrs. Prothero and the firemen.

It was on the afternoon of the day of Christmas Eve, and I was in Mrs. Prothero's garden, waiting for cats, with her son Jim. It was snowing. It was always snowing at Christmas. December, in my memory, is white as Lapland, although there were no reindeers. But there were cats. Patient, cold and callous, our hands wrapped in socks, we waited to snowball the cats. Sleek and long as jaguars and horrible-whiskered, spitting and snarling, they would slide and sidle over the white back-garden walls, and the lynx-eyed hunters, Jim and I, fur-capped and moccasined trappers from Hudson Bay, off Mumbles Road, would hurl our deadly snowballs at the green of their eyes.

The wise cats never appeared. We were so still, Eskimo-footed arctic marksmen in the muffling silence of the eternal snows—eternal, ever since Wednesday—that we never heard Mrs. Prothero's first cry from her igloo at the bottom of the garden. Or, if we heard it at all, it was, to us, like the far-off challenge of our enemy and prey, the neighbor's polar cat. But soon the voice grew louder. "Fire!" cried Mrs. Prothero, and she beat the dinner-gong.

And we ran down the garden, with the snowballs in our arms, towards the house; and smoke, indeed, was pouring out of the dining-room, and the gong was bombilating, and Mrs. Prothero was announcing ruin like a town crier in Pompeii. This was better than all the cats in Wales standing on the wall in a row. We bounded into the house, laden with snowballs, and stopped at the open door of the smoke-filled room.

Something was burning all right; perhaps it was Mr. Prothero, who always slept there after midday dinner with a newspaper over his face. But he was standing in the middle of the room, saying, "A fine Christmas!" and smacking at the smoke with a slipper.

"Call the fire brigade," cried Mrs. Prothero as she beat the gong. "They won't be here," said Mr. Prothero, "it's Christmas."

There was no fire to be seen, only clouds of smoke and Mr. Prothero standing in the middle of them, waving his slipper as though he were conducting.

"Do something," he said.

And we threw all our snowballs into the smoke—I think we missed Mr. Prothero—and ran out of the house to the telephone box.

"Let's call the police as well," Jim said.

"And the ambulance."

"And Ernie Jenkins, he likes fires."

But we only called the fire brigade, and soon the fire engine came and three tall men in helmets brought a hose into the house and Mr. Prothero got out just in time before they turned it on. Nobody could have had a noisier Christmas Eve. And when the firemen turned off the hose and were standing in the wet, smoky room, Jim's Aunt, Miss Prothero, came downstairs and peered in at them. Jim and I waited, very quietly, to hear what she would say to them. She said the right thing, always. She looked at the three tall firemen in their shining helmets, standing among the smoke and cinders and dissolving snowballs, and she said: "Would you like anything to read?"

Years and years ago, when I was a boy, when there were wolves in Wales, and birds the color of red-flannel petticoats whisked past the harp-shaped hills, when we sang and wallowed all night and day in caves that smelt like Sunday afternoons in damp front farmhouse parlors, and we chased, with the jawbones of deacons, the English and the bears, before the motor car, before the wheel, before the duchess-faced horse, when we rode the daft and happy hills bareback, it snowed and it snowed. But here a small boy says: "It snowed last year, too. I made a snowman and my brother knocked it down and I knocked my brother down and then we had tea."

"But that was not the same snow," I say. "Our snow was not only shaken from whitewash buckets down the sky, it came shawling out of the ground and swam and drifted out of the arms and hands and bodies of the trees; snow grew overnight on the roofs of the houses like a pure and grandfather moss, minutely ivied the walls and settled on the postman, opening the gate, like a dumb, numb thunderstorm of white, torn Christmas cards."

"Were there postmen then, too?"

"With sprinkling eyes and wind-cherried noses, on spread, frozen feet they crunched up to the doors and mittened on them manfully. But all that the children could hear was a ringing of bells."

"You mean that the postman went rat-a-tat-tat and the doors rang?"

"I mean that the bells that the children could hear were inside them."

"I only hear thunder sometimes, never bells."

"There were church bells, too."

"Inside them?"

"No, no, no, in the bat-black, snow-white belfries, tugged by bishops and storks. And they rang their tidings over the bandaged town, over the frozen foam of the powder and ice-cream hills, over the crackling sea. It seemed that all the churches boomed for joy under my window; and the weathercocks crew for Christmas, on our fence."

"Get back to the postmen."

"They were just ordinary postmen, fond of walking and dogs and Christmas and the snow. They knocked on the doors with blue knuckles...."

"Ours has got a black knocker...."

"And then they stood on the white Welcome mat in the little, drifted porches and huffed and puffed, making ghosts with their breath, and jogged from foot to foot like small boys wanting to go out."

"And then the presents?"

"And then the Presents, after the Christmas box. And the cold postman, with a rose on his button-nose, tingled down the tea-tray-slithered run of the chilly glinting hill. He went in his ice-bound boots like a man on fishmonger's slabs.

"He wagged his bag like a frozen camel's hump, dizzily turned the corner on one foot, and, by God, he was gone."

"Get back to the Presents."

"There were the Useful Presents: engulfing mufflers of the old coach days, and mittens made for giant sloths; zebra scarfs of a substance like silky gum that could be tug-o'-warred down to the galoshes; blinding tam-o'-shanters like patchwork tea cozies and bunny-suited busbies and balaclavas for victims of head-shrinking tribes; from aunts who always wore wool next to the skin there were mustached and rasping vests that made you wonder why the aunts had any skin left at all; and once I had a little crocheted nose bag from an aunt now, alas, no longer whinnying with us. And pictureless books in which small boys, though warned with quotations not to, *would* skate on Farmer Giles's pond and did and drowned; and books that told me everything about the wasp, except why."

"Go on to the Useless Presents."

"Bags of moist and many-colored jelly babies and a folded flag and a false nose and a tram-conductor's cap and a machine that punched tickets and rang a bell; never a catapult; once, by a mistake that no one could explain, a little hatchet; and a celluloid duck that made, when you pressed it, a most ducklike sound, a mewing moo that an ambitious cat might make who wished to be a cow; and a painting book in which I could make the grass, the trees, the sea and the animals any color I please, and still the dazzling sky-blue sheep are grazing in the red field under the rainbow-billed and pea-green birds. Hardboileds, toffee, fudge and allsorts, crunches, cracknel, humbugs, glaciers, marzipan, and butterwelsh for the Welsh. And troops of bright tin soldiers who, if they could not fight, could always run. And Snakes-and-Families and Happy Ladders. And Easy Hobbi-Games for Little Engineers, complete with instructions. Oh, easy for Leonardo! And a whistle to make the dogs bark to wake up the old man next door to make him beat on the wall with his stick to shake our picture off the wall. And a packet of cigarettes: you put one in your mouth and you stood at the corner of the street and you waited for hours, in vain, for an old lady to scold you for smoking a cigarette, and then with a smirk you ate it. And then it was breakfast under the balloons."

"Were there Uncles like in our house?"

"There are always Uncles at Christmas. The same Uncles. And on Christmas mornings, with dog-disturbing whistle and sugar fags, I would scour the swathed town for the news of the little world, and find always a dead bird by the Post Office or the white deserted swings; perhaps a robin, all but one of his fires out. Men and women wading, scooping back from chapel, with taproom noses and wind-bussed cheeks, all albinos, huddled their stiff black jarring feathers against the irreligious snow. Mistletoe hung from the gas brackets in all the front parlors; there was sherry and walnuts and bottled beer and crackers by the dessertspoons; and cats in their fur-abouts watched the fires; and the high-heaped fire spat, all ready for the chestnuts and the mulling pokers. Some few large men sat in the front parlors, without their collars, Uncles almost certainly, trying their new cigars, holding them out judiciously at arms' length, returning them to their mouths, coughing, then holding them out again as though waiting for the explosion; and some few small aunts, not wanted in the kitchen, nor anywhere else for that matter, sat on the very edges of their chairs, poised and brittle, afraid to break, like faded cups and saucers."

Not many those mornings trod the piling streets: an old man always, fawn-bowlered, yellow-gloved and, at this time of year, with spats of snow, would take his constitutional to the white bowling green and back, as he would take it wet or fire on Christmas Day or Doomsday; sometimes two hale young men, with big pipes blazing, no overcoats and wind blown scarfs, would trudge, unspeaking, down to the forlorn sea, to work up an appetite, to blow away the fumes, who knows, to walk into the waves until nothing of them was left but the two curling smoke clouds of their inextinguishable briars. Then I would be slap-dashing home, the gravy smell of the dinners of others, the bird smell, the brandy, the pudding and mince, coiling up to my nostrils, when out of a snow-clogged side lane would come a boy the spit of myself, with a pink-tipped cigarette and the violet past of a black eye, cocky as a bullfinch, leering all to himself.

I hated him on sight and sound, and would be about to put my dog whistle to my lips and blow him off the face of Christmas when suddenly he, with a violet wink, put *his* whistle to *his* lips and blew so stridently, so high, so exquisitely loud, that gobbling faces, their cheek bulged with goose, would press against their tinsled windows, the whole length of the white echoing street. For dinner we had turkey and blazing pudding, and after dinner the Uncles sat in front of the fire, loosened all buttons, put their large moist hands over their watch chains, groaned a little and slept. Mothers, aunts and sisters scuttled to and fro, bearing tureens. Aunt Bessie, who had already been frightened, twice, by a clock-work mouse, whimpered at the sideboard and had some elderberry wine. The dog was sick. Auntie Dosie had to have three aspirins, but Auntie Hannah, who liked port, stood in the middle of the snowbound back yard, singing like a big-bosomed thrush. I would blow up balloons to see how big they would blow up to; and, then when they burst, which they all did, the Uncles jumped and rumbled. In the rich and heavy afternoon, the Uncles breathing like dolphins and the snow descending, I would sit among festoons and Chinese lanterns and nibble dates and try to make a model man-o'-war, following the Instructions for Little Engineers, and produce what might be mistaken for a sea-going tramcar.

Or I would go out, my bright new boots squeaking, into the white world, on to the seaward hill, to call on Jim and Dan and Jack and to pad through the still streets, leaving huge deep footprints on the hidden pavements.

"I bet people will think there've been hippos."

"What would you do if you saw a hippo coming down our street?"

"I'd go like this, bang! I'd throw him over the railings and roll him down the hill and then I'd tickle him under the ear and he'd wag his tail."

"What would you do if you saw *two* hippos?"

Iron-flanked and bellowing he-hippos clanked and battered through the scudding snow towards us as we passed Mr. Daniel's house.

"Let's post Mr. Daniel a snowball through his letter box."

"Let's write things in the snow."

"Let's write, 'Mr. Daniel looks like a spaniel' all over his lawn."

Or we walked on the white shore. "Can the fishes see it's snowing?"

The silent one-clouded heavens drifted on to the sea. Now we were snow-blind travelers lost on the north hills, and vast dewlapped dogs, with flasks round their necks, ambled and shambled up to us, baying "Excelsior." We returned home through the poor streets where only a few children fumbled with bare red fingers in the wheel-rutted snow and cat-called after us, their voices fading away, as we trudged uphill, into the cries of the dock birds and the hooting of ships out in the whirling bay. And then, at tea the recovered Uncles would be jolly; and the ice cake loomed in the center of the table like a marble grave. Auntie Hannah laced her tea with rum, because it was only once a year.

Bring out the tall tales now that we told by the fire as the gaslight bubbled like a diver. Ghosts whooed like owls in the long nights when I dared not look over my shoulder; animals lurked in the cubbyhole under the stairs where the gas meter ticked. And I remember that we went singing carols once, when there wasn't the shaving of a moon to light the flying streets. At the end of a long road was a drive that led to a large house, and we stumbled up the darkness of the drive that night, each one of us afraid, each one holding a stone in his hand in case, and all of us too brave to say a word. The wind through the trees made noises as of old and unpleasant and maybe webfooted men wheezing in caves. We reached the black bulk of the house.

"What shall we give them? Hark the Herald?"

"No," Jack said, "Good King Wencelas. I'll count three."

One, two, three, and we began to sing, our voices high and seemingly distant in the snow-felted darkness round the house that was occupied by nobody we knew. We stood close together, near the dark door.

Good King Wencelas looked out
On the Feast of Stephen...

And then a small, dry voice, like the voice of someone who has not spoken for a long time, joined our singing: a small, dry, eggshell voice from the other side of the door: a small, dry voice through the keyhole. And when we stopped running we were outside *our* house; the front room was lovely; balloons floated under the hot-water-bottle-gulping gas; everything was good again and shone over the town.

"Perhaps it was a ghost," Jim said.

"Perhaps it was trolls," Dan said, who was always reading.

"Let's go in and see if there's any jelly left," Jack said. And we did that.

Always on Christmas night there was music. An uncle played the fiddle, a cousin sang "Cherry Ripe," and another uncle sang "Drake's Drum." It was very warm in the little house. Auntie Hannah, who had got on to the parsnip wine, sang a song about Bleeding Hearts and Death, and then another in which she said her heart was like a Bird's Nest; and then everybody laughed again; and then I went to bed. Looking through my bedroom window, out into the moonlight and the unending smoke-colored snow, I could see the lights in the windows of all the other houses on our hill and hear the music rising from them up the long, steadily falling night. I turned the gas down, I got into bed. I said some words to the close and holy darkness, and then I slept.

Portrait of the Artist as a Young Dog

The Peaches

The grass-green cart, with 'J. Jones, Gorsehill' painted shakily on it, stopped in the cobblestone passage between 'The Hare's Foot' and 'The Pure Drop.' It was late on an April evening. Uncle Jim, in his black market suit with a stiff white shirt and no collar, loud new boots, and a plaid cap, creaked and climbed down. He dragged out a thick wicker basket from a heap of straw in the corner of the cart and swung it over his shoulder. I heard a squeal from the basket and saw the tip of a pink tail curling out as Uncle Jim opened the public door of 'The Pure Drop.'

'I won't be two minutes,' he said to me. The bar was full; two fat women in bright dresses sat near the door, one with a small, dark child on her knee; they saw Uncle Jim and nudged up on the bench.

'I'll be out straight away,' he said fiercely, as though I had contradicted him, 'you stay there quiet.'

The woman without the child raised up her hands. 'Oh, Mr Jones,' she said in a high laughing voice. She shook like a jelly.

Then the door closed and the voices were muffled.

I sat alone on the shaft of the cart in the narrow passage, staring through a side window of 'The Hare's Foot.' A stained blind was drawn half over it. I could see into half of a smoky, secret room, where four men were playing cards. One man was huge and swarthy, with a handlebar moustache and a love-curl on his forehead; seated by his side was a thin, bald, pale old man with his cheeks in his mouth; the faces of the other two were in shadow. They all drank out of brown pint tankards and never spoke, laying the cards down with a smack, scraping at their match-boxes, puffing at their pipes, swallowing unhappily, ringing the brass bell, ordering more, by a sign of the fingers, from a sour woman with a flowered blouse and a man's cap.

The passage grew dark too suddenly, the walls crowded in, and the roofs crouched down. To me, staring timidly there in a dark passage in a strange town, the swarthy man appeared like a giant in a cage surrounded by clouds, and the bald old man withered into a black hump with a white top; two white hands darted out of the corner with invisible cards. A man with spring-heeled boots and a two-edged knife might be bouncing towards me from Union Street.

I called, 'Uncle Jim, Uncle Jim,' softly so that he should not hear.

I began to whistle between my teeth, but when I stopped I thought the sound went hissing on behind me. I climbed down from the shaft and stepped close to the half-blind window; a hand clawed up the pane to the tassel of the blind; in the little, packed space between me on the cobbles and the card-players at the table, I could not tell which side of the glass was the hand that dragged the blind down slowly. I was cut from the night by a stained square. A story I had made in the warm, safe island of my bed, with sleepy midnight Swansea flowing and rolling round outside the house, came blowing down to me then with a noise on the cobbles. I remembered the demon in the story, with his wings and hooks, who clung like a bat to my hair as I battled up and down Wales after a tall, wise, golden, royal girl from Swansea Convent. I tried to remember her true name, her proper, long, black-stockinged legs, her giggle and paper curls, but the hooked wings tore at me and the colour of her hair and eyes faded and vanished like the grass-green of the cart that was a dark, grey mountain now standing between the passage walls.

And all this time the old, broad, patient, nameless mare stood without stirring, not stamping once on the cobbles or shaking her reins. I called her a good girl and stood on tiptoe to try to stroke her ears as the door of 'The Pure Drop' swung open and the warm lamplight from the bar dazzled me and burned my story up. I felt frightened no longer, only angry and hungry. The two fat women near the door giggled 'Good night, Mr Jones' out of the rich noise and the comfortable smells. The child lay curled asleep under the bench. Uncle Jim kissed the two women on the lips.

'Good night.'

'Good night.'

'Good night.'

Then the passage was dark again.

He backed the mare into Union Street, lurching against her side, cursing her patience and patting her nose, and we both climbed into the cart.

'There are too many drunken gipsies,' he said as we rolled and rattled through the flickering, lamp-lit town.

He sang hymns all the way to Gorsehill in an affectionate bass voice, and conducted the wind with his whip. He did not need to touch the reins. Once on the rough road, between hedges twisting out to twig the mare by the bridle and poke our caps, we stopped, at a whispered 'Whoa,' for uncle to light his pipe and set the darkness on fire and show his long, red, drunken, fox's face to me, with its bristling side-bushes and wet, sensitive nose. A white house with a light in one bedroom window shone in a field on a short hill beyond the road.

Uncle whispered, 'Easy, easy, girl,' to the mare, though she was standing calmly, and said to me over his shoulder in a suddenly loud voice: 'A hangman lived there.'

He stamped on the shaft, and we rattled on through a cutting wind. Uncle shivered, pulling down his cap to hide his ears; but the mare was like a clumsy statue trotting, and all the demons of my stories, if they trotted by her side or crowded together and grinned into her eyes, would not make her shake her head or hurry.

'I wish he'd have hung Mrs Jesus,' uncle said.

Between hymns he cursed the mare in Welsh. The white house was left behind, the light and the hill were swallowed up.

'Nobody lives there now,' he said.

We drove into the farm-yard of Gorsehill, where the cobbles rang and the black, empty stables took up the ringing and hollowed it so that we drew up in a hollow circle of darkness and the mare was a hollow animal and nothing lived in the hollow house at the end of the yard but two sticks with faces scooped out of turnips.

'You run and see Annie,' said uncle. 'There'll be hot broth and potatoes.'

He led the hollow, shaggy statue towards the stable; clop, clop to the mice-house. I heard locks rattle as I ran to the farm-house door.

The front of the house was the single side of a black shell, and the arched door was the listening ear. I pushed the door open and walked into the passage out of the wind. I might have been walking into the hollow night and the wind, passing through a tall vertical shell on an inland sea-shore. Then a door at the end of the passage opened; I saw the plates on the shelves, the lighted lamp on the long, oil-clothed table, 'Prepare to Meet Thy God' knitted over the fire-place, the smiling china dogs, the brown-stained settle, the grandmother clock, and I ran into the kitchen and into Annie's arms.

There was a welcome, then. The clock struck twelve as she kissed me, and I stood among the shining and striking like a prince taking off his disguise. One minute I was small and cold, skulking dead-scared down a black passage in my stiff, best suit, with my hollow belly thumping and my heart like a time bomb, clutching my grammar school cap, unfamiliar to myself, a snub-nosed story-teller lost in his own adventures and longing to be home; the next I was a royal nephew in smart town clothes, embraced and welcomed, standing in the snug centre of my stories and listening to the clock announcing me. She hurried me to the seat in the side of the cavernous fire-place and took off my shoes. The bright lamps and the ceremonial gongs blazed and rang for me.

She made a mustard bath and strong tea, told me to put on a pair of my cousin Gwilym's socks and an old coat of uncle's that smelt of rabbit and tobacco. She fussed and clucked and nodded and told me, as she cut bread and butter, how Gwilym was still studying to be a minister, and how Aunt Rach Morgan, who was ninety years old, had fallen on her belly on a scythe.

Then Uncle Jim came in like the devil with a red face and a wet nose and trembling, hairy hands. His walk was thick. He stumbled against the dresser and shook the coronation plates, and a lean cat shot booted out from the settle corner. Uncle looked nearly twice as tall as Annie. He could have carried her about under his coat and brought her out suddenly, a little, brown-skinned, toothless, hunchbacked woman with a cracked, sing-song voice.

'You shouldn't have kept him out so long,' she said, angry and timid.

He sat down in his special chair, which was the broken throne of a bankrupt bard, and lit his pipe and stretched his legs and puffed clouds at the ceiling.

'He might catch his death of cold,' she said.

She talked at the back of his head while he wrapped himself in clouds. The cat slunk back. I sat at the table with my supper finished, and found a little empty bottle and a white balloon in the pockets of my coat.

'Run off to bed, there's a dear,' Annie whispered.

'Can I go and look at the pigs?'

'In the morning, dear,' she said.

So I said good night to Uncle Jim, who turned and smiled at me and winked through the smoke, and I kissed Annie and lit my candle.

'Good night.'

'Good night.'

'Good night.'

I climbed the stairs; each had a different voice. The house smelt of rotten wood and damp and animals. I thought that I had been walking long, damp passages all my life, and climbing stairs in the dark, alone. I stopped outside Gwilym's door on the draughty landing.

'Good night.'

The candle flame jumped in my bedroom where a lamp was burning very low, and the curtains waved; the water in a glass on a round table by the bed stirred, I thought, as the door closed, and lapped against the sides. There was a stream below the window; I thought it lapped against the house all night until I slept.

'Can I go and see the pigs?' I asked Gwilym next morning. The hollow fear of the house was gone, and, running downstairs to my breakfast, I smelt the sweetness of wood and the fresh spring grass and the quiet untidy farm-yard, with its tumbledown dirty-white cow-house and empty stables open.

Gwilym was a tall young man aged nearly twenty, with a thin stick of a body and spade-shaped face. You could dig the garden with him. He had a deep voice that cracked in half when he was excited, and he sang songs to himself, treble and bass, with the same sad hymn tune, and wrote hymns in the barn. He told me stories about girls who died for love. 'And she put a rope round a tree but it was too short,' he said; 'she stuck a penknife in her bosoms but it was too blunt.' We were sitting together on the straw heaps that day in the half-dark of the shuttered stable. He twisted and leaned near to me, raising his big finger, and the straw creaked.

'She jumped in the cold river, she jumped,' he said, his mouth against my ear, 'arse over tip and, Diu, she was dead.' He squeaked like a bat.

The pigsties were at the far end of the yard. We walked towards them, Gwilym dressed in minister's black, though it was a weekday morning, and me in a serge suit with a darned bottom, past three hens scrabbling the muddy cobbles and a collie with one eye, sleeping with it open. The ramshackle outhouses had tumbling, rotten roofs, jagged holes in their sides, broken shutters, and peeling whitewash; rusty screws ripped out from the dangling, crooked boards; the lean cat of the night before sat snugly between the splintered jaws of bottles, cleaning its face, on the tip of the rubbish pile that rose triangular and smelling sweet and strong to the level of the riddled cart-house roof. There was nowhere like that farm-yard in all the slapdash county, nowhere so poor and grand and dirty as that square of mud and rubbish and bad wood and falling stone, where a bucketful of old and bedraggled hens scratched and laid small eggs. A duck quacked out of the trough in one deserted sty. Now a young man and a curly boy stood staring and sniffing over a wall at a sow, with its tits on the mud, giving suck.

'How many pigs are there?'

'Five. The bitch ate one,' said Gwilym.

We counted them as they squirmed and wriggled, rolled on their backs and bellies, edged and pinched and pushed and squealed about their mother. There were four. We counted again. Four pigs, four naked pink tails curling up as their mouths guzzled down and the sow grunted with pain and joy.

'She must have ate another,' I said, and picked up a scratching stick and prodded the grunting sow and rubbed her crusted bristles backwards. 'Or a fox jumped over the wall,' I said.

'It wasn't the sow or the fox,' said Gwilym. 'It was father.'

I could see uncle, tall and sly and red, holding the writhing pig in his two hairy hands, sinking his teeth in its thigh, crunching its trotters up; I could see him leaning over the wall of the sty with the pig's legs sticking out of his mouth. 'Did Uncle Jim eat the pig?'

Now, at this minute, behind the rotting sheds, he was standing, knee-deep in feathers, chewing off the live heads of the poultry.

'He sold it to go on the drink,' said Gwilym in his deepest rebuking whisper, his eyes fixed on the sky. 'Last Christmas he took a sheep over his shoulder, and he was pissed for ten days.'

The sow rolled nearer the scratching stick, and the small pigs sucking at her, lost and squealing in the sudden darkness, struggled under her folds and pouches.

'Come and see my chapel,' said Gwilym. He forgot the lost pig at once and began to talk about the towns he had visited on a religious tour, Neath and Bridgend and Bristol and Newport, with their lakes and luxury gardens, their bright, coloured streets roaring with temptation. We walked away from the sty and the disappointed sow.

'I met actress after actress,' he said.

Gwilym's chapel was the last old barn before the field that led down to the river; it stood well above the farm-yard, on a mucky hill. There was one whole door with a heavy padlock, but you could get in easily through the holes on either side of it. He took out a ring of keys and shook them gently and tried each one in the lock. 'Very posh,' he said; 'I bought them from the junk-shop in Carmarthen.' We climbed into the chapel through a hole.

A dusty wagon with the name painted out and a whitewash cross on its side stood in the middle. 'My pulpit cart,' he said, and walked solemnly into it up the broken shaft. 'You sit on the hay; mind the mice,' he said. Then he brought out his deepest voice again, and cried to the heavens and the bat-lined rafters and the hanging webs: 'Bless us this holy day, O Lord, bless me and Dylan and this Thy little chapel for ever and ever, Amen. I've done a lot of improvements to this place.'

I sat on the hay and stared at Gwilym preaching, and heard his voice rise and crack and sink to a whisper and break into singing and Welsh and ring triumphantly and be wild and meek. The sun, through a hole, shone on his praying shoulders, and he said: 'O God, Thou art everywhere all the time, in the dew of the morning, in the frost of the evening, in the field and the town, in the preacher and the sinner, in the sparrow and the big buzzard. Thou canst see everything, right down deep in our hearts; Thou canst see us when the sun is gone; Thou canst see us when there aren't any stars, in the gravy blackness, in the deep, deep, deep, deep pit; Thou canst see and spy and watch us all the time, in the little black corners, in the big cowboys' prairies, under the blankets when we're snoring fast, in the terrible shadows, pitch black, pitch black; Thou canst see everything we do, in the night and the day, in the day and the night, everything, everything; Thou canst see all the time. O God, mun, you're like a bloody cat.'

He let his clasped hands fall. The chapel in the barn was still, and shafted with sunlight. There was nobody to cry Hallelujah or God-bless; I was too small and enamoured in the silence. The one duck quacked outside.

'Now I take a collection,' Gwilym said.

He stepped down from the cart and groped about in the hay beneath it and held out a battered tin to me.

'I haven't got a proper box,' he said.

I put two pennies in the tin.

'It's time for dinner,' he said, and we went back to the house without a word.

Annie said, when we had finished dinner: 'Put on your nice suit for this afternoon. The one with stripes.'

It was to be a special afternoon, for my best friend, Jack Williams, from Swansea, was coming down with his rich mother in a motor car, and Jack was to spend a fortnight's holiday with me.

'Where's Uncle Jim?'

'He's gone to market,' said Annie.

Gwilym made a small pig's noise. We knew where uncle was; he was sitting in a public house with a heifer over his shoulder and two pigs nosing out of his pockets, and his lips were wet with bull's blood.

'Is Mrs Williams very rich?' asked Gwilym.

I told him she had three motor cars and two houses, which was a lie. 'She's the richest woman in Wales, and once she was a mayoress,' I said. 'Are we going to have tea in the best room?'

Annie nodded. 'And a large tin of peaches,' she said.

'That old tin's been in the cupboard since Christmas,' said Gwilym, 'mother's been keeping it for a day like this.'

'They're lovely peaches,' Annie said. She went upstairs to dress like Sunday.

The best room smelt of mothballs and fur and damp and dead plants and stale, sour air. Two glass cases on wooden coffin-boxes lined the window wall. You looked at the weed-grown vegetable garden through a stuffed fox's legs, over a partridge's head, along the red-paint-stained breast of a stiff wild duck. A case of china and pewter, trinkets, teeth, family brooches, stood beyond the bandy table; there was a large oil lamp on the patchwork table-cloth, a Bible with a clasp, a tall vase with a draped woman about to bathe on it, and a framed photograph of Annie, Uncle Jim, and Gwilym smiling in front of a fern-pot. On the mantelpiece were two clocks, some dogs, brass candlesticks, a shepherdess, a man in a kilt, and a tinted photograph of Annie, with high hair and her breasts coming out. There were chairs around the table and in each corner, straight, curved, stained, padded, all with lace cloths hanging over their backs. A patched white sheet shrouded the harmonium. The fire-place was full of brass tongs, shovels, and pokers. The best room was rarely used. Annie dusted and brushed and polished there once a week, but the carpet still sent up a grey cloud when you trod on it, and dust lay evenly on the seats of the chairs, and balls of cotton and dirt and black stuffing and long black horse hairs were wedged in the cracks of the sofa. I blew on the glass to see the pictures. Gwilym and castles and cattle.

'Change your suit now,' said Gwilym.

I wanted to wear my old suit, to look like a proper farm boy and have manure in my shoes and hear it squelch as I walked, to see a cow have calves and a bull on top of a cow, to run down in the dingle and wet my stockings, to go out and shout, 'Come on, you b——,' and pelt the hens and talk in a proper voice. But I went upstairs to put my striped suit on.

From my bedroom I heard the noise of a motor car drawing up in the yard. It was Jack Williams and his mother.

Gwilym shouted, 'They're here, in a Daimler!' from the foot of the stairs, and I ran down to meet them with my tie undone and my hair uncombed.

Annie was saying at the door: 'Good afternoon, Mrs Williams, good afternoon. Come right in, it's a lovely day, Mrs Williams. Did you have a nice journey then? This way, Mrs Williams, mind the step.'

Annie wore a black, shining dress that smelt of mothballs, like the chair covers in the best room; she had forgotten to change her gymshoes, which were caked with mud and all holes. She fussed on before Mrs Williams down the stone passage, darting her head round, clucking, fidgeting, excusing the small house, anxiously tidying her hair with one rough, stubby hand.

Mrs Williams was tall and stout, with a jutting bosom and thick legs, her ankles swollen over her pointed shoes; she was fitted out like a mayoress or a ship, and she swayed after Annie into the best room.

She said: 'Please don't put yourself out for me, Mrs Jones, there's a dear.' She dusted the seat of a chair with a lace handkerchief from her bag before sitting down.

'I can't stop, you know,' she said.

'Oh, you must stay for a cup of tea,' said Annie, shifting and scraping the chairs away from the table so that nobody could move and Mrs Williams was hemmed in fast with her bosom and her rings and her bag, opening the china cupboard, upsetting the Bible on the floor, picking it up, dusting it hurriedly with her sleeve.

'And peaches,' Gwilym said. He was standing in the passage with his hat on.

Annie said, 'Take your hat off, Gwilym, make Mrs Williams comfortable,' and she put the lamp on the shrouded harmonium and spread out a white table-cloth that had a tea stain in the centre, and brought out the china and laid knives and cups for five.

'Don't bother about me, there's a dear,' said Mrs Williams. 'There's a lovely fox!' She flashed a finger of rings at the glass case.

'It's real blood,' I told Jack, and we climbed over the sofa to the table.

'No it isn't,' he said, 'it's red ink.'

'Oh, your shoes!' said Annie.

'Don't tread on the sofa, Jack, there's a dear.'

'If it isn't ink it's paint then.'

Gwilym said: 'Shall I get you a bit of cake, Mrs Williams?'

Annie rattled the tea-cups. 'There isn't a single bit of cake in the house,' she said; 'we forgot to order it from the shop; not a single bit. Oh, Mrs Williams!'

Mrs Williams said: 'Just a cup of tea, thanks.' She was still sweating because she had walked all the way from the car. It spoiled her powder. She sparkled her rings and dabbed at her face.

'Three lumps,' she said. 'And I'm sure Jack will be very happy here.'

'Happy as sandboys.' Gwilym sat down.

'Now, you must have some peaches, Mrs Williams, they're lovely.'

'They should be, they've been here long enough,' said Gwilym.

Annie rattled the tea-cups at him again.

'No peaches, thanks,' Mrs Williams said.

'Oh, you must, Mrs Williams, just one. With cream.'

'No, no, Mrs Jones, thanks the same,' she said. 'I don't mind pears or chunks, but I can't bear peaches.'

Jack and I had stopped talking. Annie stared down at her gymshoes. One of the two clocks on the mantelpiece coughed, and struck. Mrs Williams struggled from her chair.

'There, time flies!' she said.

She pushed her way past the furniture, jostled against the cupboard, rattled the trinkets and brooches, and kissed Jack on the forehead.

'You've got scent on,' he said.

She patted my head.

'Now, behave yourselves.'

To Annie, she said in a whisper: 'And remember, Mrs Jones, just good plain food. No spoiling his appetite.'

Annie followed her out of the room. She moved slowly now. 'I'll do my very best, Mrs Williams.'

We heard her say, 'Good-bye then, Mrs Williams,' and go down the steps of the kitchen and close the door. The motor car roared in the yard, then the noise grew softer and died.

Down the thick dingle Jack and I ran shouting, scalping the brambles with our thin stick-hatchets, dancing, hallooing. We skidded to a stop and prowled on the bushy banks of the stream. Up above, sat one-eyed, dead-eyed, sinister, slim, ten-notched Gwilym, loading his guns in Gallows Farm. We crawled and rat-tatted through the bushes, hid, at a whistled signal, in the deep grass, and crouched there, waiting for the crack of a twig or the secret breaking of boughs.

On my haunches, eager and alone, casting an ebony shadow, with the Gorsehill jungle swarming, the violent, impossible birds and fishes leaping, hidden under four-stemmed flowers the height of horses, in the early evening in a dingle near Carmarthen, my friend Jack Williams invisibly near me, I felt all my young body like an excited animal surrounding me, the torn knees bent, the bumping heart, the long heat and depth between the legs, the sweat prickling in the hands, the tunnels down to the eardrums, the little balls of dirt between the toes, the eyes in the sockets, the tucked-up voice, the blood racing, the memory around and within flying, jumping, swimming, and waiting to pounce. There, playing Indians in the evening, I was aware of me myself in the exact middle of a living story, and my body was my adventure and my name. I sprang with excitement and scrambled up through the scratching brambles again.

Jack cried: 'I see you! I see you!' He scampered after me. 'Bang! bang! you're dead!'

But I was young and loud and alive, though I lay down obediently.

'Now you try and kill me,' said Jack. 'Count a hundred.'

I closed one eye, saw him rush and stamp towards the upper field, then tiptoe back and begin to climb a tree, and I counted fifty and ran to the foot of the tree and killed him as he climbed. 'You fall down,' I said.

He refused to fall, so I climbed too, and we clung to the top branches and stared down at the lavatory in the corner of the field. Gwilym was sitting on the seat with his trousers down. He looked small and black. He was reading a book and moving his hands.

'We can see you!' we shouted.

He snatched his trousers up and put the book in his pocket.

'We can see you, Gwilym!'

He came out into the field. 'Where are you, then?'

We waved our caps at him.

'In the sky!' Jack shouted.

'Flying!' I shouted.

We stretched our arms out like wings.

'Fly down here.'

We swung and laughed on the branches.

'There's birds!' cried Gwilym.

Our jackets were torn and our stockings were wet and our shoes were sticky; we had green moss and brown bark on our hands and faces when we went in for supper and a scolding. Annie was quiet that night, though she called me a ragamuffin and said she didn't know what Mrs Williams would think and told Gwilym he should know better. We made faces at Gwilym and put salt in his tea, but after supper he said: 'You can come to chapel if you like. Just before bed.'

He lit a candle on the top of the pulpit cart. It was a small light in the big barn. The bats were gone. Shadows still clung upside down along the roof. Gwilym was no longer my cousin in a Sunday suit, but a tall stranger shaped like a spade in a cloak, and his voice grew too deep. The straw heaps were lively. I thought of the sermon on the cart: we were watched, Jack's heart was watched, Gwilym's tongue was marked down, my whisper, 'Look at the little eyes,' was remembered always.

'Now I take confessions,' said Gwilym from the cart.

Jack and I stood bareheaded in the circle of the candle, and I could feel the trembling of Jack's body.

'You first.' Gwilym's finger, as bright as though he had held it in the candle flame until it burned, pointed me out, and I took a step towards the pulpit cart, raising my head.

'Now you confess,' said Gwilym.

'What have I got to confess?'

'The worst thing you've done.'

I let Edgar Reynolds be whipped because I had taken his homework; I stole from my mother's bag; I stole from Gwyneth's bag; I stole twelve books in three visits from the library, and threw them away in the park; I drank a cup of my water to see what it tasted like; I beat a dog with a stick so that it would roll over and lick my hand afterwards; I looked with Dan Jones through the keyhole while his maid had a bath; I cut my knee with a penknife, and put the blood on my handkerchief and said it had come out of my ears so that I could pretend I was ill and frighten my mother; I pulled my trousers down and showed Jack Williams; I saw Billy Jones beat a pigeon to death with a fire-shovel, and laughed and got sick; Cedric Williams and I broke into Mrs Samuels's house and poured ink over the bed-clothes.

I said: 'I haven't done anything bad.'

'Go on, confess!' said Gwilym. He was frowning down at me.

'I can't! I can't!' I said. 'I haven't done anything bad.'

'Go on, confess!'

'I won't! I won't!'

Jack began to cry. 'I want to go home,' he said.

Gwilym opened the chapel door and we followed him into the yard, down past the black, humped sheds, towards the house, and Jack sobbed all the way.

In bed together, Jack and I confessed our sins.

'I steal from my mother's bag, too; there are pounds and pounds.'

'How much do you steal?'

'Threepence.'
'I killed a man once.'
'No you didn't then.'
'Honest to Christ, I shot him through the heart.'
'What was his name?'
'Williams.'
'Did he bleed?'
I thought the stream was lapping against the house.
'Like a bloody pig,' I said.
Jack's tears had dried. 'I don't like Gwilym, he's barmy.'
'No, he isn't. I found a lot of poems in his bedroom once. They were all written to girls. And he showed them to me afterwards, and he'd changed all the girls' names to God.'
'He's religious.'
'No he isn't, he goes with actresses. He knows Corinne Griffith.'
Our door was open. I liked the door locked at night, because I would rather have a ghost in the bedroom than think of one coming in; but Jack liked it open, and we tossed and he won. We heard the front door rattle and footsteps in the kitchen passage.
'That's Uncle Jim.'
'What's he like?'
'He's like a fox, he eats pigs and chickens.'
The ceiling was thin and we heard every sound, the creaking of the bard's chair, the clatter of plates, Annie's voice saying: 'Midnight!'
'He's drunk,' I said. We lay quite still, hoping to hear a quarrel.
'Perhaps he'll throw plates,' I said.
But Annie scolded him softly: 'There's a fine state, Jim.'
He murmured to her.
'There's one pig gone,' she said. 'Oh, why do you have to do it, Jim? There's nothing left now. We'll never be able to carry on.'
'Money! money! money!' he said. I knew he would be lighting his pipe.

Then Annie's voice grew so soft we could not hear the words, and uncle said: 'Did she pay you the thirty shillings?'

'They're talking about your mother,' I told Jack.

For a long time Annie spoke in a low voice, and we waited for words. 'Mrs Williams,' she said, and 'motor car,' and 'Jack,' and 'peaches.' I thought she was crying, for her voice broke on the last word.

Uncle Jim's chair creaked again, he might have struck his fist on the table, and we heard him shout: 'I'll give her peaches! Peaches, peaches! Who does she think she is? Aren't peaches good enough for her? To hell with her bloody motor car and her bloody son! Making us small.'

'Don't, don't, Jim!' Annie said, 'you'll wake the boys.'

'I'll wake them and whip the hell out of them, too!'

'Please, please, Jim!'

'You send the boy away,' he said, 'or I'll do it myself. Back to his three bloody houses.'

Jack pulled the bed-clothes over his head and sobbed into the pillow: 'I don't want to hear, I don't want to hear. I'll write to my mother. She'll take me away.'

I climbed out to close the door. Jack would not talk to me again, and I fell asleep to the noise of the voices below, which soon grew gentle.

Uncle Jim was not at breakfast. When we came down, Jack's shoes were cleaned for him and his jacket was darned and pressed. Annie gave two boiled eggs to Jack and one to me. She forgave me when I drank tea from the saucer.

After breakfast, Jack walked to the post office. I took the one-eyed collie to chase rabbits in the upper fields, but it barked at ducks and brought me a tramp's shoe from a hedge, and lay down with its tail wagging in a rabbit hole. I threw stones at the deserted duck pond, and the collie ambled back with sticks.

Jack went skulking into the damp dingle, his hands in his pockets, his cap over one eye. I left the collie sniffing at a molehill, and climbed to the tree-top in the corner of the lavatory field. Below me, Jack was playing Indians all alone, scalping through the bushes, surprising himself round a tree, hiding from himself in the grass. I called to him once, but he pretended not to hear. He played alone, silently and savagely. I saw him standing with his hands in his pockets, swaying like a Kelly, on the mud-bank by the stream at the foot of the dingle. My bough lurched, the heads of the dingle bushes spun up towards me like green tops, 'I'm falling!' I cried, my trousers saved me, I swung and grasped, this was one minute of wild adventure, but Jack did not look up and the minute was lost. I climbed, without dignity, to the ground.

Early in the afternoon, after a silent meal, when Gwilym was reading the scriptures or writing hymns to girls or sleeping in his chapel, Annie was baking bread, and I was cutting a wooden whistle in the loft over the stable, the motor car drove up in the yard again.

Out of the house Jack, in his best suit, ran to meet his mother, and I heard him say as she stepped, raising her short skirts, on to the cobbles: 'And he called you a bloody cow, and he said he'd whip the hell out of me, and Gwilym took me to the barn in the dark and let the mice run over me, and Dylan's a thief, and that old woman's spoilt my jacket.'

Mrs Williams sent the chauffeur for Jack's luggage. Annie came to the door, trying to smile and curtsy, tidying her hair, wiping her hands on her pinafore.

Mrs Williams said, 'Good afternoon,' and sat with Jack in the back of the car and stared at the ruin of Gorsehill.

The chauffeur came back. The car drove off, scattering the hens. I ran out of the stable to wave to Jack. He sat still and stiff by his mother's side. I waved my handkerchief.

A Visit to Grandpa's

In the middle of the night I woke from a dream full of whips and lariats as long as serpents, and runaway coaches on mountain passes, and wide, windy gallops over cactus fields, and I heard the old man in the next room crying, 'Gee-up!' and 'Whoa!' and trotting his tongue on the roof of his mouth.

It was the first time I had stayed in grandpa's house. The floorboards had squeaked like mice as I climbed into bed, and the mice between the walls had creaked like wood as though another visitor was walking on them. It was a mild summer night, but curtains had flapped and branches beaten against the window. I had pulled the sheets over my head, and soon was roaring and riding in a book.

'Whoa there, my beauties!' cried grandpa. His voice sounded very young and loud, and his tongue had powerful hooves, and he made his bedroom into a great meadow. I thought I would see if he was ill, or had set his bed-clothes on fire, for my mother had said that he lit his pipe under the blankets, and had warned me to run to his help if I smelt smoke in the night. I went on tiptoe through the darkness to his bedroom door, brushing against the furniture and upsetting a candlestick with a thump. When I saw there was a light in the room I felt frightened, and as I opened the door I heard grandpa shout, 'Gee-up!' as loudly as a bull with a megaphone.

He was sitting straight up in bed and rocking from side to side as though the bed were on a rough road; the knotted edges of the counterpane were his reins; his invisible horses stood in a shadow beyond the bed-side candle. Over a white flannel nightshirt he was wearing a red waistcoat with walnut-sized brass buttons. The over-filled bowl of his pipe smouldered among his whiskers like a little, burning hayrick on a stick. At the sight of me, his hands dropped from the reins and lay blue and quiet, the bed stopped still on a level road, he muffled his tongue into silence, and the horses drew softly up.

'Is there anything the matter, grandpa?' I asked, though the clothes were not on fire. His face in the candlelight looked like a ragged quilt pinned upright on the black air and patched all over with goat-beards.

He stared at me mildly. Then he blew down his pipe, scattering the sparks and making a high, wet dog-whistle of the stem, and shouted: 'Ask no questions.'

After a pause, he said slyly: 'Do you ever have nightmares, boy?'

I said: 'No.'

'Oh, yes, you do,' he said.

I said I was woken by a voice that was shouting to horses.

'What did I tell you?' he said. 'You eat too much. Who ever heard of horses in a bedroom?'

He fumbled under his pillow, brought out a small, tinkling bag, and carefully untied its strings. He put a sovereign in my hand, and said: 'Buy a cake.' I thanked him and wished him good night.

As I closed my bedroom door, I heard his voice crying loudly and gaily, 'Gee-up! gee-up!' and the rocking of the travelling bed.

In the morning I woke from a dream of fiery horses on a plain that was littered with furniture, and of large, cloudy men who rode six horses at a time and whipped them with burning bed-clothes. Grandpa was at breakfast, dressed in deep black. After breakfast he said, 'There was a terrible loud wind last night,' and sat in his arm-chair by the hearth to make clay balls for the fire. Later in the morning he took me for a walk, through Johnstown village and into the fields on the Llanstephan road.

A man with a whippet said, 'There's a nice morning, Mr Thomas,' and when he had gone, leanly as his dog, into the short-treed green wood he should not have entered because of the notices, grandpa said: 'There, do you hear what he called you? Mister!'

We passed by small cottages, and all the men who leant on the gates congratulated grandpa on the fine morning. We passed through the wood full of pigeons, and their wings broke the branches as they rushed to the tops of the trees. Among the soft, contented voices and the loud, timid flying, grandpa said, like a man calling across a field: 'If you heard those old birds in the night, you'd wake me up and say there were horses in the trees.'

We walked back slowly, for he was tired, and the lean man stalked out of the forbidden wood with a rabbit held as gently over his arm as a girl's arm in a warm sleeve.

On the last day but one of my visit I was taken to Llanstephan in a governess cart pulled by a short, weak pony. Grandpa might have been driving a bison, so tightly he held the reins, so ferociously cracked the long whip, so blasphemously shouted warning to boys who played in the road, so stoutly stood with his gaitered legs apart and cursed the demon strength and wilfulness of his tottering pony.

'Look out, boy!' he cried when we came to each corner, and pulled and tugged and jerked and sweated and waved his whip like a rubber sword. And when the pony had crept miserably round each corner, grandpa turned to me with a sighing smile: 'We weathered that one, boy.'

When we came to Llanstephan village at the top of the hill, he left the cart by the 'Edwinsford Arms' and patted the pony's muzzle and gave it sugar, saying: 'You're a weak little pony, Jim, to pull big men like us.'

He had strong beer and I had lemonade, and he paid Mrs Edwinsford with a sovereign out of the tinkling bag; she inquired after his health, and he said that Llangadock was better for the tubes. We went to look at the churchyard and the sea, and sat in the wood called the Sticks, and stood on the concert platform in the middle of the wood where visitors sang on midsummer nights and, year by year, the innocent of the village was elected mayor. Grandpa paused at the churchyard and pointed over the iron gate at the angelic headstones and the poor wooden crosses. 'There's no sense in lying there,' he said.

We journeyed back furiously: Jim was a bison again.

I woke late on my last morning, out of dreams where the Llanstephan sea carried bright sailing-boats as long as liners; and heavenly choirs in the Sticks, dressed in bards' robes and brass-buttoned waistcoats, sang in a strange Welsh to the departing sailors. Grandpa was not at breakfast; he rose early. I walked in the fields with a new sling, and shot at the Towy gulls and the rooks in the parsonage trees. A warm wind blew from the summer points of the weather; a morning mist climbed from the ground and floated among the trees and hid the noisy birds; in the mist and the wind my pebbles flew lightly up like hailstones in a world on its head. The morning passed without a bird falling.

I broke my sling and returned for the midday meal through the parson's orchard. Once, grandpa told me, the parson had bought three ducks at Carmarthen Fair and made a pond for them in the centre of the garden; but they waddled to the gutter under the crumbling doorsteps of the house, and swam and quacked there. When I reached the end of the orchard path, I looked through a hole in the hedge and saw that the parson had made a tunnel through the rockery that was between the gutter and the pond and had set up a notice in plain writing: 'This way to the pond.'

The ducks were still swimming under the steps.

Grandpa was not in the cottage. I went into the garden, but grandpa was not staring at the fruit-trees. I called across to a man who leant on a spade in the field beyond the garden hedge: 'Have you seen my grandpa this morning?'

He did not stop digging, and answered over his shoulder: 'I seen him in his fancy waistcoat.'

Griff, the barber, lived in the next cottage. I called to him through the open door: 'Mr Griff, have you seen my grandpa?'

The barber came out in his shirtsleeves.

I said: 'He's wearing his best waistcoat.' I did not know if it was important, but grandpa wore his waistcoat only in the night.

'Has grandpa been to Llanstephan?' asked Mr Griff anxiously.

'We went there yesterday in a little trap,' I said.

He hurried indoors and I heard him talking in Welsh, and he came out again with his white coat on, and he carried a striped and coloured walking-stick. He strode down the village street and I ran by his side.

When we stopped at the tailor's shop, he cried out, 'Dan!' and Dan Tailor stepped from his window where he sat like an Indian priest but wearing a derby hat. 'Dai Thomas has got his waistcoat on,' said Mr Griff, 'and he's been to Llanstephan.'

As Dan Tailor searched for his overcoat, Mr Griff was striding on. 'Will Evans,' he called outside the carpenter's shop, 'Dai Thomas has been to Llanstephan, and he's got his waistcoat on.'

'I'll tell Morgan now,' said the carpenter's wife out of the hammering, sawing darkness of the shop.

We called at the butcher's shop and Mr Price's house, and Mr Griff repeated his message like a town crier.

We gathered together in Johnstown square. Dan Tailor had his bicycle, Mr Price his pony trap. Mr Griff, the butcher, Morgan Carpenter, and I climbed into the shaking trap, and we trotted off towards Carmarthen town. The tailor led the way, ringing his bell as though there were a fire or a robbery, and an old woman by the gate of a cottage at the end of the street ran inside like a pelted hen. Another woman waved a bright handkerchief.

'Where are we going?' I asked.

Grandpa's neighbours were as solemn as old men with black hats and jackets on the outskirts of a fair. Mr Griff shook his head and mourned: 'I didn't expect this again from Dai Thomas.'

'Not after last time,' said Mr Price sadly.

We trotted on, we crept up Constitution Hill, we rattled down into Lammas Street, and the tailor still rang his bell and a dog ran, squealing, in front of his wheels. As we clip-clopped over the cobbles that led down to the Towy bridge, I remembered grandpa's nightly noisy journeys that rocked the bed and shook the walls, and I saw his gay waistcoat in a vision and his patchwork head tufted and smiling in the candlelight. The tailor before us turned round on his saddle, his bicycle wobbled and skidded. 'I see Dai Thomas!' he cried.

The trap rattled on to the bridge, and I saw grandpa there; the buttons of his waistcoat shone in the sun, he wore his tight, black Sunday trousers and a tall, dusty hat I had seen in a cupboard in the attic, and he carried an ancient bag. He bowed to us. 'Good morning, Mr Price,' he said, 'and Mr Griff and Mr Morgan and Mr Evans.' To me, he said: 'Good morning, boy.'

Mr Griff pointed his coloured stick at him.

'And what do you think you are doing on Carmarthen bridge in the middle of the afternoon,' he said sternly, 'with your best waistcoat and your old hat?'

Grandpa did not answer, but inclined his face to the river wind, so that his beard was set dancing and wagging as though he talked, and watched the coracle men move, like turtles, on the shore.

Mr Griff raised his stunted barber's pole. 'And where do you think you are going,' he said, 'with your old black bag?'

Grandpa said: 'I am going to Llangadock to be buried.' And he watched the coracle shells slip into the water lightly, and the gulls complain over the fish-filled water as bitterly as Mr Price complained:

'But you aren't dead yet, Dai Thomas.'

For a moment grandpa reflected, then: 'There's no sense in lying dead in Llanstephan,' he said. 'The ground is comfy in Llangadock; you can twitch your legs without putting them in the sea.'

His neighbours moved close to him. They said: 'You aren't dead, Mr Thomas.'

'How can you be buried, then?'

'Nobody's going to bury you in Llanstephan.'

'Come on home, Mr Thomas.'

'There's strong beer for tea.'

'And cake.'

But grandpa stood firmly on the bridge, and clutched his bag to his side, and stared at the flowing river and the sky, like a prophet who has no doubt.

Patricia, Edith, and Arnold

The small boy in his invisible engine, the Cwmdonkin Special, its wheels, polished to dazzle, crunching on the small back garden scattered with breadcrumbs for the birds and white with yesterday's snow, its smoke rising thin and pale as breath in the cold afternoon, hooted under the wash-line, kicked the dog's plate at the washhouse stop, and puffed and pistoned slower and slower while the servant girl lowered the pole, unpegged the swinging vests, showed the brown stains under her arms, and called over the wall: 'Edith, Edith, come here, I want you.'

Edith climbed on two tubs on the other side of the wall and called back: 'I'm here, Patricia.' Her head bobbed up above the broken glass.

He backed the Flying Welshman from the washhouse to the open door of the coal-hole and pulled hard on the brake that was a hammer in his pocket; assistants in uniform ran out with fuel; he spoke to a saluting fireman, and the engine shuffled off, round the barbed walls of China that kept the cats away, by the frozen rivers in the sink, in and out of the coal-hole tunnel. But he was listening carefully all the time, through the squeals and whistles, to Patricia and the next-door servant, who belonged to Mrs Lewis, talking when they should have been working, calling his mother Mrs T., being rude about Mrs L.

He heard Patricia say: 'Mrs T. won't be back till six.'

And Edith next door replied: 'Old Mrs L. has gone to Neath to look for Mr Robert.'

'He's on the randy again,' Patricia whispered.

'Randy, sandy, bandy!' cried the boy out of the coal-hole.

'You get your face dirty, I'll kill you,' Patricia said absent-mindedly.

She did not try to stop him when he climbed up the coal-heap. He stood quietly on the top, King of the Coal Castle, his head touching the roof, and listened to the worried voices of the girls. Patricia was almost in tears, Edith was sobbing and rocking on the unsteady tubs. 'I'm standing on the top of the coal,' he said, and waited for Patricia's anger.

She said: 'I don't want to see him, you go alone.'

'We must, we must go together,' said Edith. 'I've got to know.'

'I don't want to know.'

'I can't stand it, Patricia, you must go with me.'

'You go alone, he's waiting for you.'

'Please, Patricia!'

'I'm lying on my face in the coal,' said the boy.

'No, it's your day with him. I don't want to know. I just want to think he loves me.'

'Oh, talk sense, Patricia, please! Will you come or no? I've got to hear what he says.'

'All right then, in half an hour. I'll shout over the wall.'

'You'd better come soon,' the boy said, 'I'm dirty as Christ knows what.'

Patricia ran to the coal-hole. 'The language! Come out of there at once!' she said.

The tubs began to slide and Edith vanished.

'Don't you dare use language like that again. Oh! your suit!' Patricia took him indoors.

She made him change his suit in front of her. 'Otherwise there's no telling.' He took off his trousers and danced around her, crying: 'Look at me, Patricia!'

'You be decent,' she said, 'or I won't take you to the park.'

'Am I going to the park, then?'

'Yes, we're all going to the park; you and me and Edith next door.'

He dressed himself neatly, not to annoy her, and spat on his hands before parting his hair. She appeared not to notice his silence and neatness. Her large hands were clasped together; she stared down at the white brooch on her chest. She was a tall, thick girl with awkward hands, her fingers were like toes, her shoulders were wide as a man's.

'Am I satisfactory?' he asked.

'There's a long word,' she said, and looked at him lovingly. She lifted him up and seated him on the top of the chest of drawers. 'Now you're as tall as I am.'

'But I'm not so old,' he said.

He knew that this was an afternoon on which anything might happen; it might snow enough for sliding on a tray; uncles from America, where he had no uncles, might arrive with revolvers and St Bernards; Ferguson's shop might catch on fire and all the piece-packets fall on the pavements; and he was not surprised when she put her black, straight-haired, heavy head on his shoulder and whispered into his collar: 'Arnold, Arnold Matthews.'

'There, there,' he said, and rubbed her parting with his finger and winked at himself in the mirror behind her and looked down her dress at the back.

'Are you crying?'

'No.'

'Yes you are, I can feel the wet.'

She dried her eyes on her sleeve. 'Don't you let on that I was crying.'

'I'll tell everybody, I'll tell Mrs T. and Mrs L., I'll tell the policeman and Edith and my dad and Mr Chapman, Patricia was crying on my shoulder like a nanny goat, she cried for two hours, she cried enough to fill a kettle. I won't really,' he said.

As soon as he and Patricia and Edith set off for the park, it began to snow. Big flakes unexpectedly fell on the rocky hill, and the sky grew dark as dusk though it was only three in the afternoon. Another boy, somewhere in the allotments behind the houses, shouted as the first flakes fell. Mrs Ocky Evans opened the top bay-window of Springmead and thrust her head and hands out, as though to catch the snow. He waited, without revolt, for Patricia to say, 'Quick! hurry back, it's snowing!' and to pack him in out of the day before his feet were wet. Patricia can't have seen the snow, he thought at the top of the hill, though it was falling heavily, sweeping against her face, covering her black hat.

He dared not speak, for fear of waking her, as they turned the corner into the road that led down to the park. He lagged behind to take his cap off and catch the snow in his mouth.

'Put on your cap,' said Patricia, turning. 'Do you want to catch your death of cold?'

She tucked his muffler inside his coat, and said to Edith: 'Will he be there in the snow, do you think? He's bound to be there, isn't he? He was always there on my Wednesdays, wet or fine.' The tip of her nose was red, her cheeks glowed like coals, she looked handsomer in the snow than in the summer, when her hair would lie limp on her wet forehead and a warm patch spread on her back.

'He'll be there,' Edith said. 'One Friday it was pelting down and he was there. He hasn't got anywhere else to go, he's always there. Poor Arnold!' She looked white and tidy in a coat with a fur piece, and twice as small as Patricia; she stepped through the thick snow as though she were going shopping.

'Wonders will never cease,' he said aloud to himself. This was Patricia letting him walk in the snow, this was striding along in a storm with two big girls. He sat down in the road. 'I'm on a sledge,' he said, 'pull me, Patricia, pull me like an Eskimo.'

'Up you get, you moochin, or I'll take you home.'

He saw that she did not mean it. 'Lovely Patricia, beautiful Patricia,' he said, 'pull me along on my bottom.'

'Any more dirty words, and you know who I'll tell.'

'Arnold Matthews,' he said.

Patricia and Edith drew closer together.

'He notices everything,' Patricia whispered.

Edith said: 'I'm glad I haven't got your job.'

'Oh,' said Patricia, catching him by the hand and pressing it on her arm, 'I wouldn't change him for the world!'

He ran down the gravel path on to the upper walk of the park. 'I'm spoilt!' he shouted, 'I'm spoilt! Patricia spoils me!'

Soon the park would be white all over; already the trees were blurred round the reservoir and fountain, and the training college on the gorse hill was hidden in a cloud. Patricia and Edith took the steep path down to the shelter. Following on the forbidden grass, he slid past them straight into a bare bush, but the bump and the pricks left him shouting and unhurt. The girls gossiped sadly now. They shook their coats in the deserted shelter, scattering snow on the seats, and sat down, close together still, outside the bowling-club window.

'We're only just on time,' said Edith. 'It's hard to be punctual in the snow.'

'Can I play by here?'

Patricia nodded. 'Play quietly then; don't be rough with the snow.'

'Snow! snow! snow!' he said, and scooped it out of the gutter and made a small ball.

'Perhaps he's found a job,' Patricia said.

'Not Arnold.'

'What if he doesn't come at all?'

'He's bound to come, Patricia; don't say things like that.'

'Have you brought your letters?'

'They're in my bag. How many have you got?'

'No, how many have you got, Edith?'

'I haven't counted.'

'Show me one of yours,' Patricia said.

He was used to their talk by this time; they were old and cuckoo, sitting in the empty shelter sobbing over nothing. Patricia was reading a letter and moving her lips.

'He told me that, too,' she said, 'that I was his star.'

'Did he begin: "Dear Heart?"'

'Always: "Dear Heart."'

Edith broke into real, loud tears. With a snowball in his hand, he watched her sway on the seat and hide her face in Patricia's snowy coat.

Patricia said, patting and calming Edith, rocking her head: 'I'll give him a piece of my mind when he comes!'

When who comes? He threw the snowball high into the silently driving fall. Edith's crying in the deadened park was clear and thin as a whistle, and, disowning the soft girls and standing away from them in case a stranger passed, a man with boots to his thighs, or a sneering, bigger boy from the Uplands, he piled the snow against the wire of the tennis court and thrust his hands into the snow like a baker making bread. As he delved and moulded the snow into loaves, saying under his breath, 'This is the way it is done, ladies and gentlemen,' Edith raised her head and said: 'Patricia, promise me, don't be cross with him. Let's all be quiet and friendly.'

'Writing, "Dear Heart" to us both,' said Patricia angrily. 'Did he ever take off your shoes and pull your toes and——'

'No, no, you mustn't, don't go on, you mustn't speak like that!' Edith put her fingers to her cheeks. 'Yes, he did,' she said.

'Somebody has been pulling Edith's toes,' he said to himself, and ran round the other side of the shelter, chuckling. 'Edith went to market,' he laughed aloud, and stopped at the sight of a young man without an overcoat sitting in a corner seat and cupping his hands and blowing into them. The young man wore a white muffler and a check cap. When he saw the boy, he pulled his cap down over his eyes. His hands were pale blue and the ends of his fingers yellow.

The boy ran back to Patricia. 'Patricia, there's a man!' he cried.

'Where's a man?'

'On the other side of the shelter; he hasn't got an overcoat and he's blowing in his hands like this.'

Edith jumped up. 'It's Arnold!'

'Arnold Matthews, Arnold Matthews, we know you're there!' Patricia called round the shelter, and, after a long minute, the young man, raising his cap and smiling, appeared at the corner and leant against a wooden pillar.

The trousers of his sleek blue suit were wide at the bottoms; the shoulders were high and hard, and sharp at the ends; his pointed patent shoes were shining; a red handkerchief stuck from his breast pocket; he had not been out in the snow.

'Fancy you two knowing each other,' he said loudly, facing the red-eyed girls and the motionless, open-mouthed boy who stood at Patricia's side with his pockets full of snowballs.

Patricia tossed her head and her hat fell over one eye. As she straightened her hat, 'You come and sit down here, Arnold Matthews, you've got some questions to answer!' she said in her washing-day voice.

Edith clutched at her arm: 'Oh! Patricia you promised.' She picked at the edge of her handkerchief. A tear rolled down her cheek.

Arnold said softly then: 'Tell the little boy to run away and play.'

The boy ran round the shelter once and returned to hear Edith saying, 'There's a hole in your elbow, Arnold,' and to see the young man kicking the snow at his feet and staring at the names and hearts cut on the wall behind the girls' heads.

'Who did you walk out with on Wednesdays?' Patricia asked. Her clumsy hands held Edith's letter close to the sprinkled folds of her chest.

'You, Patricia.'

'Who did you walk out with on Fridays?'

'With Edith, Patricia.'

He said to the boy: 'Here, son, can you roll a snowball as big as a football?'

'Yes, as big as two footballs.'

Arnold turned back to Edith, and said: 'How did you come to know Patricia Davies? You work in Brynmill.'

'I just started working in Cwmdonkin,' she said. 'I haven't seen you since, to tell you. I was going to tell you to-day, but I found out. How could you, Arnold? Me on my afternoon off, and Patricia on Wednesdays.'

The snowball had turned into a short snow man with a lop-sided, dirty head and a face full of twigs, wearing a boy's cap and smoking a pencil.

'I didn't mean any harm,' said Arnold. 'I love you both.'

Edith screamed. The boy jumped forward, and the snow man with a broken back collapsed.

'Don't tell your lies, how can you love two of us?' Edith cried, shaking her handbag at Arnold. The bag snapped open, and a bundle of letters fell on the snow.

'Don't you dare pick up those letters,' Patricia said.

Arnold had not moved. The boy was searching for his pencil in the snow man's ruins.

'You make your choice, Arnold Matthews, here and now.'

'Her or me,' said Edith.

Patricia turned her back to him. Edith, with her bag in her hand hanging open, stood still. The sweeping snow turned up the top page of a letter.

'You two,' he said, 'you go off the handle. Sit down and talk. Don't cry like that, Edith. Hundreds of men love more than one woman, you're always reading about it. Give us a chance, Edith, there's a girl.'

Patricia looked at the hearts and arrows and old names. Edith saw the letters curl.

'It's you, Patricia,' said Arnold.

Still Patricia stood turned away from him. Edith opened her mouth to cry, and he put a finger to his lips. He made the shape of a whisper, too soft for Patricia to hear. The boy watched him soothing and promising Edith, but she screamed again and ran out of the shelter and down the path, her handbag beating against her side.

'Patricia,' he said, 'turn round to me. I had to say it. It's you, Patricia.'

The boy bent down over the snow man and found his pencil driven through its head. When he stood up he saw Patricia and Arnold arm in arm.

Snow dripped through his pockets, snow melted in his shoes, snow trickled down his collar into his vest. 'Look at you now,' said Patricia, rushing to him and holding him by the hands, 'you're wringing wet.'

'Only a bit of snow,' said Arnold, suddenly alone in the shelter.

'A bit of snow indeed, he's cold as ice and his feet are like sponges. Come on home at once!'

The three of them climbed the path to the upper walk, and Patricia's footprints were large as a horse's in the thickening snow.

'Look, you can see our house, it's got a white roof!'

'We'll be there, ducky, soon.'

'I'd rather stay out and make a snow man like Arnold Matthews.'

'Hush! hush! your mother'll be waiting. You must come home.'

'No she won't. She's gone on a randy with Mr Robert. Randy, sandy, bandy!'

'You know very well she's shopping with Mrs Partridge, you mustn't tell wicked lies.'

'Well Arnold Matthews told lies. He said he loved you better than Edith, and he whispered behind your back to her.'

'I swear I didn't, Patricia, I don't love Edith at all!'

Patricia stopped walking. 'You don't love Edith?'

'No, I've told you, it's you. I don't love her at all,' he said. 'Oh! my God, what a day! Don't you believe me? It's you, Patricia. Edith isn't anything. I just used to meet her; I'm always in the park.'

'But you told her you loved her.'

The boy stood bewildered between them. Why was Patricia so angry and serious? Her face was flushed and her eyes shone. Her chest moved up and down. He saw the long black hairs on her leg through a tear in her stocking. Her leg is as big as my middle, he thought. I'm cold; I want tea; I've got snow in my fly.

Arnold backed slowly down the path. 'I had to tell her that or she wouldn't have gone away. I had to, Patricia. You saw what she was like. I hate her. Cross my heart!'

'Bang! bang!' cried the boy.

Patricia was smacking Arnold, tugging at his muffler, knocking him with her elbows. She pummelled him down the path, and shouted at the top of her voice: 'I'll teach you to lie to Edith! You pig! you black! I'll teach you to break her heart!'

He shielded his face from her blows as he staggered back. 'Patricia, Patricia, don't hit me! There's people!'

As Arnold fell, two women with umbrellas up peered through the whirling snow from behind a bush.

Patricia stood over him. 'You lied to her and you'd lie to me,' she said. 'Get up, Arnold Matthews!'

He rose and set his muffler straight and wiped his eyes with the red handkerchief, and raised his cap and walked towards the shelter.

'And as for you,' Patricia said, turning to the watching women, 'you should be ashamed of yourselves! Two old women playing about in the snow.'

They dodged behind the bush.

Patricia and the boy climbed, hand in hand, back to the upper walk.

'I've left my cap by the snow man,' he remembered. 'It's my cap with the Tottenham colours.'

'Run back quickly,' she said, 'you can't get any wetter than you are.'

He found his cap half hidden under snow. In a corner of the shelter, Arnold sat reading the letters that Edith had dropped, turning the wet pages slowly. He did not see the boy, and the boy, behind a pillar, did not interrupt him. Arnold read every letter carefully.

'You've been a long time finding your cap,' Patricia said. 'Did you see the young man?'

'No,' he said, 'he was gone.'

At home, in the warm living-room, Patricia made him change his clothes again. He held his hands in front of the fire, and soon they began to hurt.

'My hands are on fire,' he told her, 'and my toes, and my face.'

After she had comforted him, she said: 'There, that's better. The hurting's gone. You won't call the king your uncle in a minute.' She was bustling about the room. 'Now we've all had a good cry to-day.'

The Fight

I was standing at the end of the lower playground and annoying Mr Samuels, who lived in the house just below the high railings. Mr Samuels complained once a week that boys from the school threw apples and stones and balls through his bedroom window. He sat in a deck chair in a small square of trim garden and tried to read the newspaper. I was only a few yards from him. I was staring him out. He pretended not to notice me, but I knew he knew I was standing there rudely and quietly. Every now and then he peeped at me from behind his newspaper, saw me still and serious and alone, with my eyes on his. As soon as he lost his temper I was going to go home. Already I was late for dinner. I had almost beaten him, the newspaper was trembling, he was breathing heavily, when a strange boy, whom I had not heard approach, pushed me down the bank.

I threw a stone at his face. He took off his spectacles, put them in his coat pocket, took off his coat, hung it neatly on the railings, and attacked. Turning round as we wrestled on the top of the bank, I saw that Mr Samuels had folded his newspaper on the deck chair and was standing up to watch us. It was a mistake to turn round. The strange boy rabbit-punched me twice. Mr Samuels hopped with excitement as I fell against the railings. I was down in the dust, hot and scratched and biting, then up and dancing, and I butted the boy in the belly and we tumbled in a heap. I saw through a closing eye that his nose was bleeding. I hit his nose. He tore at my collar and spun me round by the hair.

'Come on! come on!' I heard Mr Samuels cry.

We both turned towards him. He was shaking his fists and dodging about in the garden. He stopped then, and coughed, and set his panama straight, and avoided our eyes, and turned his back and walked slowly to the deck chair.

We both threw gravel at him.

'I'll give him "Come on!"' the boy said, as we ran along the playground away from the shouts of Mr Samuels and down the steps on to the hill.

We walked home together. I admired his bloody nose. He said that my eye was like a poached egg, only black.

'I've never seen such a lot of blood,' I said.

He said I had the best black eye in Wales, perhaps it was the best black eye in Europe; he bet Tunney never had a black eye like that.

'And there's blood all over your shirt.'

'Sometimes I bleed in dollops,' he said.

On Walter's Road we passed a group of high school girls, and I cocked my cap and hoped my eye was as big as a bluebag, and he walked with his coat flung open to show the bloodstains.

I was a hooligan all during dinner, and a bully, and as bad as a boy from the Sandbanks, and I should have more respect, and I sat silently, like Tunney, over the sago pudding. That afternoon I went to school with an eyeshade on. If I had had a black silk sling I would have been as gay and desperate as the wounded captain in the book that my sister used to read, and that I read under the bed-clothes at night, secretly with a flash-lamp.

On the road, a boy from an inferior school, where the parents did not have to pay anything, called me 'One eye!' in a harsh, adult voice. I took no notice, but walked along whistling, my good eye on the summer clouds sailing, beyond insult, above Terrace Road.

The mathematics master said: 'I see that Mr Thomas at the back of the class has been straining his eyesight. But it isn't over his homework, is it, gentlemen?'

Gilbert Rees, next to me, laughed loudest.

'I'll break your leg after school!' I said.

He'd hobble, howling, up to the head master's study. A deep hush in the school. A message on a plate brought by the porter. 'The head master's compliments, sir, and will you come at once?' 'How did you happen to break this boy's leg?' 'Oh! damn and bottom, the agony!' cried Gilbert Rees. 'Just a little twist,' I would say. 'I don't know my own strength. I apologize. But there's nothing to worry about. Let me set the leg, sir.' A rapid manipulation, the click of a bone. 'Doctor Thomas, sir, at your service.' Mrs Rees was on her knees. 'How can I thank you?' 'It's nothing at all, dear lady. Wash his ears every morning. Throw away his rulers. Pour his red and green inks down the sink.'

In Mr Trotter's drawing class we drew naked girls inaccurately on sheets of paper under our drawings of a vase and passed them along under the desks. Some of the drawings were detailed strangely, others were tailed off like mermaids. Gilbert Rees drew the vase only.

'Sleep with your wife, sir?'

'What did you say?'

'Lend me a knife, sir?'

'What would you do if you had a million pounds?'

'I'd buy a Bugatti and a Rolls and a Bentley and I'd go two hundred miles an hour on Pendine sands.'

'I'd buy a harem and keep the girls in the gym.'

'I'd buy a house like Mrs Cotmore-Richard's, twice as big as hers, and a cricket field and a football field and a proper garage with mechanics and a lift.'

'And a lavatory as big as, as big as the Melba pavilion, with plush seats and golden chains and . . .'

'And I'd smoke cigarettes with real gold tips, better than Morris's Blue Book.'

'I'd buy all the railway trains, and only 4A could travel in them.'

'And not Gilbert Rees either.'

'What's the longest you've been?'

'I went to Edinburgh.'

'My father went to Salonika in the War.'

'Where's that, Cyril?'

'Cyril, tell us about Mrs Pussie Edwards in Hanover Street.'

'Well, my brother says he can do anything.'

I drew a wild guess below the waist, and wrote Pussie Edwards in small letters at the foot of the page.

'Cave!'

'Hide your drawings.'

'I bet you a greyhound can go faster than a horse.'

Everybody liked the drawing class, except Mr Trotter.

In the evening, before calling on my new friend, I sat in my bedroom by the boiler and read through my exercise-books full of poems. There were Danger Don'ts on the backs. On my bedroom walls were pictures of Shakespeare, Walter de la Mare torn from my father's Christmas *Bookman*, Robert Browning, Stacy Aumonier, Rupert Brooke, a bearded man who I had discovered was Whittier, Watts's 'Hope,' and a Sunday school certificate I was ashamed to want to pull down. A poem I had had printed in the 'Wales Day by Day' column of the *Western Mail* was pasted on the mirror to make me blush, but the shame of the poem had died. Across the poem I had written, with a stolen quill and in flourishes: 'Homer Nods.' I was always waiting for the opportunity to bring someone into my bedroom—'Come into my den; excuse the untidiness; take a chair. No! not that one, it's broken!'—and force him to see the poem accidentally. 'I put it there to make me blush.' But nobody ever came in except my mother.

Walking to his house in the early dusk through solid, deserted professional avenues lined with trees, I recited pieces of my poems and heard my voice, like a stranger's voice in Park Drive accompanied by the tap-tapping of nailed boots, rise very thinly up through the respectable autumn evening.

'My mind is fashioned
In the ways of intertissue;
Veiled and passioned
Are the thoughts that issue
From its well of furtive lust

Raptured by the devil's dust.'

If I looked through a window on to the road, I would see a scarlet-capped boy with big boots striding down the middle, and would wonder who it could be. If I were a young girl watching, my face like Mona Lisa's, my coal-black hair coiled in earphones, I'd see beneath the 'Boys' Department' suit a manly body with hair and sun tan, and call him and ask, 'Will you have tea or cocktails?' and hear his voice reciting the *Grass Blade's Psalm* in the half-dark of the heavily curtained and coloured drawing-room hung about with famous reproductions and glowing with books and wine bottles:

'The frost has lain,
Frost that is dark with flowered slain,
Fragilely strewn
With patches of illuminated moon,
About my lonely head in flagged unlovely red.
'The frost has spake,
Frost secretive and thrilled in silent flake,
With unseen lips of blue
Glass in the glaze stars threw,
Only to my ears, has spake in visionary tears.
'The frost has known,
From scattered conclave by the few winds blown,
That the lone genius in my roots,
Bare down there in a jungle of fruits,
Has planted a green year, for praise, in the heart of my upgrowing days.
'The frost has filled
My heart with longing that the night's sleeve spilled,
Frost of celestial vapour fraught,
Frost that the columns of unfallen snow have sought,
With desire for the fields of space hovering about my single place.'
'Look! there's a strange boy, walking alone like a prince.'

'No, no, like a wolf! Look at his long stride!' Sketty church was shaking its bells for me.

'When I am strewn low
And all my ashes are
Dust in a dumb provoking show
Of minatory star...'

I recited. A young man and woman, arm in arm, suddenly appeared from a back lane between houses. I changed my recitation into a tune and hummed past them. They would be tittering together now, with their horrid bodies close. Cissy, moony, long hair. I whistled hard and loud, kicked a tradesmen's entrance, and glanced back over my shoulder. The couple were gone. Here's a kick at 'The Elms.' 'Where are the bleedy elms, mister?' Here's a handful of gravel, Mrs 'The Croft,' right at your window. One night I would paint 'Bum' all over the front gate of 'Kia-Ora.'

A woman stood on 'Lyndhurst' steps with a hissing pom, and, stuffing my cap in my pocket, I was off down the road; and there was Dan's house, 'Warmley,' with music coming loudly out of it.

He was a composer and a poet too; he had written seven historical novels before he was twelve, and he played the piano and the violin; his mother made wool pictures, his brother was a clerk at the docks and syncopated, his aunt kept a preparatory school on the first floor, and his father wrote music for the organ. All this he had told me as we walked home bleeding, strutting by the gym-frocks, waving to boys in the trams.

My new friend's mother answered the door with a ball of wool in her hand. Dan, in the upstairs drawing-room, heard my arrival and played the piano faster.

'I didn't hear you come in,' he said when I found him. He finished on a grand chord, stretching all his fingers.

The room was splendidly untidy, full of wool and paper and open cupboards stacked with things you could never find; all the expensive furniture had been kicked; a waistcoat hung on the chandelier. I thought I could live for ever in that room, writing and fighting and spilling ink, having my friends for picnics there after midnight with Waller's rum-and-butter and charlottes russes from Eynon's, and Cydrax and Vino.

He showed me his books and his seven novels. All the novels were about battles, sieges, and kings. 'Just early stuff,' he said.

He let me take out his violin and make a cat noise.

We sat on a sofa in the window and talked as though we had always known each other. Would the 'Swans' beat the 'Spurs'? When could girls have babies? Was Arnott's average last year better than Clay's?

'That's my father outside there on the road,' he said, 'the tall one waving his arms.'

Two men were talking on the tram-lines. Mr Jenkyn looked as if he were trying to swim down Eversley Road, he breast-stroked the air and beat on the ground with his feet, and then he limped and raised one shoulder higher than the other.

'Perhaps he's describing a fight,' I said.

'Or telling Mr Morris a story about cripples,' said Dan. 'Can you play the piano?'

'I can do chords, but not tunes,' I said.

We played a duet with crossed hands.

'Now who's that sonata by?'

We made a Dr Percy, who was the greatest composer for four hands in the world, and I was Paul America, the pianist, and Dan was Winter Vaux.

I read him an exercise-book full of poems. He listened wisely, like a boy aged a hundred, his head on one side and his spectacles shaking on his swollen nose. 'This is called *Warp*,' I said:

'Like suns red from running tears,
Five suns in the glass,
Together, separate yet, yet separately round,

Red perhaps, but the glass is as pale as grass,
Glide, without sound.
In unity, five tears lid-awake, suns yet, but salt,
Five inscrutable spears in the head,
Each sun but an agony,
Twist perhaps, pain bled of hate,
Five into one, the one made of five into one, early
Suns distorted to late.
All of them now, madly and desolate,
Spun with the cloth of the five, run
Widely and foaming, wildly and desolate,
Shoot through and dive. One of the five is the sun.'

The noise of the trains past the house clattered away as far as the sea or farther, into the dredgered bay. Nobody had ever listened like that before. The school had vanished, leaving on Mount Pleasant hill a deep hole that smelt of cloakrooms and locker mice, and 'Warmley' shone in the dark of a town I did not know. In the still room, that had never been strange to me, sitting in heaps of coloured wool, swollen-nosed and one-eyed, we acknowledged our gifts. The future spread out beyond the window, over Singleton Park crowded with lovers messing about, and into smoky London paved with poems.

Mrs Jenkyn peered round the door and switched the light on. 'There, that's more homely,' she said. 'You aren't cats.'

The future went out with the light, and we played a thumping piece by Dr Percy—'Have you ever heard anything so beautiful? Louder, louder, America!' said Dan. 'Leave a bit of bass for me,' I said—until the next-door wall was rapped.

'That's the Careys. Mr Carey's a Cape Horner,' Dan said.

We played him one harsh, whaling piece before Mrs Jenkyn, with wool and needles, ran upstairs.

When she had gone, Dan said: 'Why is a man always ashamed of his mother?'

'Perhaps he isn't when he's older,' I said, but I doubted it. The week before I was walking down High Street with three boys after school, and I saw my mother with a Mrs Partridge outside the Kardomah. I knew she would stop me in front of the others and say, 'Now you be home early for tea,' and I wanted High Street to open and suck me down. I loved her and disowned her. 'Let's cross over,' I said, 'there's some sailors' boots in Griffith's window.' But there was only a dummy with a golf suit on, and a roll of tweed.

'Supper isn't for half an hour yet. What shall we do?'
'Let's see who can hold that chair up the longest,' I said.
'No, let's edit a paper; you do the literature, I'll do the music.'
'What shall we call it, then?'

He wrote, '*The* ——, edited by D. Jenkyn and D. Thomas,' on the back of a hat-box from under the sofa. The rhythm was better with D. Thomas and D. Jenkyn, but it was his house.

'What about *The Maestersingers*?'
'No, that's too musical,' I said.
'*The Warmley Magazine?*'
'No,' I said, 'I live in "Glanrhyd."'

After the hat-box was covered, we wrote,
'*The Thunderer*, edited by D. Jenkyn' Thomas'
in chalk on a piece of cardboard and pinned it on the wall.

'Would you like to see our maid's bedroom?' asked Dan. We whispered up to the attic.
'What's her name?'
'Hilda.'
'Is she young?'
'No, she's twenty or thirty.'

Her bed was untidy. 'My mother says you can always smell a maid.' We smelled the sheets. 'I can't smell anything.'

In her brass-bound box was a framed photograph of a young man wearing plus-fours.

'That's her boy.'

'Let's give him a moustache.'

Somebody moved downstairs, a voice called, 'Supper now!' and we hurried out, leaving the box open. 'One night we'll hide under her bed,' Dan said as we opened the dining-room door.

Mr Jenkyn, Mrs Jenkyn, Dan's aunt, and a Reverend Bevan and Mrs Bevan were seated at the table.

Mr Bevan said grace. When he stood up, it was just as though he were still sitting down, he was so short. 'Bless our repast this evening,' he said, as though he didn't like the food at all. But once 'Amen' was over, he went at the cold meat like a dog.

Mrs Bevan didn't look all there. She stared at the table-cloth and made hesitant movements with her knife and fork. She appeared to be wondering which to cut up first, the meat or the cloth.

Dan I stared at her with delight; he kicked me under the table and I spilt the salt. In the commotion I managed to put some vinegar on his bread.

Mrs Jenkyn said, while every one except Mr Bevan was watching Mrs Bevan moving her knife slowly along the edge of her plate: 'I do hope you like cold lamb.'

Mrs Bevan smiled at her, assured, and began to eat. She was grey-haired and grey-faced. Perhaps she was grey all over. I tried to undress her, but my mind grew frightened when it came to her short flannel petticoat and navy bloomers to the knees. I couldn't even dare unbutton her tall boots to see how grey her legs were. She looked up from her plate and gave me a wicked smile.

Blushing, I turned to answer Mr Jenkyn, who was asking me how old I was. I told him, but added one year. Why did I lie then? I wondered. If I lost my cap and found it in my bedroom, and my mother asked me where I had found it, I would say, 'In the attic,' or, 'Under the hall stand.' It was exciting to have to keep wary all the time in case I contradicted myself, to make up the story of a film I pretended to have seen and put Jack Holt in Richard Dix's place.

'Fifteen and three-quarters,' said Mr Jenkyns, 'that's a very exact age. I see we have a mathematician with us. Now see if he can do this little sum.'

He finished his supper and laid out matches on the plate.

'That's an old one, dad,' Dan said.

'Oh, I'd like to see it very much,' I said in my best voice. I wanted to come to the house again. This was better than home, and there was a woman off her head, too.

When I failed to place the matches rightly, Mr Jenkyn showed me how it was done, and, still not understanding, I thanked him and asked him for another one. It was almost as good being a hypocrite as being a liar; it made you warm and shameful.

'What were you talking to Mr Morris about in the street, dad?' asked Dan. 'We saw you from upstairs.'

'I was telling him how the Swansea and District Male Voice did the *Messiah*, that's all. Why do you ask?'

Mr Bevan couldn't eat any more, he was full. For the first time since supper began, he looked round the table. He didn't seem to like what he saw. 'How are studies progressing, Daniel?'

'Listen to Mr Bevan, Dan, he's asking you a question.'

'Oh, so so.'

'So so?'

'I mean they're going very well, thank you, Mr Bevan.'

'Young people should attempt to say what they mean.'

Mrs Bevan giggled, and asked for more meat. 'More meat,' she said.

'And you, young man, have you a mathematical bent?'

'No, sir,' I said, 'I like English.'

'He's a poet,' said Dan, and looked uncomfortable.

'A brother poet,' Mr Bevan corrected, showing his teeth.

'Mr Bevan has published books,' said Mr Jenkyn. '*Proserpine, Psyche*——'

'*Orpheus*,' said Mr Bevan sharply.

'And *Orpheus*. You must show Mr Bevan some of your verses.'

'I haven't got anything with me, Mr Jenkyn.'

'A poet,' said Mr Bevan, 'should carry his verses in his head.'

'I remember them all right,' I said.

'Recite me your latest one; I'm always very interested.'

'What a gathering,' Mrs Jenkyn said, 'poets, musicians, preachers. We only want a painter now, don't we?'

'I don't think you'll like the very latest one,' I said.

'Perhaps,' said Mr Bevan, smiling, 'I am the best judge of that.'

'Frivolous is my hate,' I said, wanting to die, watching Mr Bevan's teeth,

'Singed with bestial remorse
Of unfulfilment of desired force,
And lust of tearing late;
'Now could I raise
Her dead, dark body to my own
And hear the joyous rustle of her bone
And in her eyes see deathly blaze;
'Now could I wake
To passion after death, and taste
The rapture of her hating, tear the waste
Of body. Break, her dead, dark body, break.'

Dan kicked my shins in the silence before Mr Bevan said: 'The influence is obvious, of course. "Break, break, break, on thy cold, grey stones, O sea."'

'Hubert knows Tennyson backwards,' said Mrs Bevan, 'backwards.'

'Can we go upstairs now?' Dan asked.

'No annoying Mr Carey then.'

And we shut the door softly behind us and ran upstairs with our hands over our mouths.

'Damn! damn! damn!' said Dan. 'Did you see the reverend's face?'

We imitated him up and down the room, and had a short fight on the carpet. Dan's nose began to bleed again. 'That's nothing, it'll stop in a minute. I can bleed when I like.'

'Tell me about Mrs Bevan. Is she mad?'

'She's terribly mad, she doesn't know who she is. She tried to throw herself out of the window but he didn't take any notice, so she came up to our house and told mother all about it.'

Mrs Bevan knocked and walked in. 'I hope I'm not interrupting you.'

'No, of course not, Mrs Bevan.'

'I wanted a little change of air,' she said. She sat down in the wool on the sofa by the window.

'Isn't it a close night?' said Dan. 'Would you like the window open?'

She looked at the window.

'I can easily open it for you,' Dan said, and winked at me.

'Let me open it for you, Mrs Bevan,' I said.

'It's good to have the window open.'

'And this is a nice high window too.'

'Plenty of air from the sea.'

'Let it be, dear,' she said, 'I'll just sit here and wait for my husband.'

She played with the balls of wool, picked up a needle and tapped it gently on the palm of her hand.

'Is Mr Bevan going to be long?'

'I'll just sit and wait for my husband,' she said.

We talked to her some more about windows, but she only smiled and undid the wool, and once she put the blunt end of the long needle in her ear. Soon we grew tired of watching her, and Dan played the piano—'My twentieth sonata,' he said, 'this one is *Homage to Beethoven*'—and at half-past nine I had to go home.

I said good night to Mrs Bevan, who waved the needle and bowed sitting down, and Mr Bevan downstairs gave me his cold hand to shake, and Mr and Mrs Jenkyn told me to come again, and the quiet aunt gave me a Mars bar.

'I'll send you a bit of the way,' said Dan.

Outside, on the pavement, in the warm night, we looked up at the lighted drawing-room window. It was the only light in the road.

'Look! there she is!'

Mrs Bevan's face was pressed against the glass, her hook nose flattened, her lips pressed tight, and we ran all the way down Eversley Road in case she jumped.

At the corner, Dan said: 'I must leave you now, I've got to finish a string trio to-night.'

'I'm working on a long poem,' I said, 'about the princes of Wales and the wizards and everybody.'

We both went home to bed.

Extraordinary Little Cough

One afternoon, in a particularly bright and glowing August, some years before I knew I was happy, George Hooping, whom we called Little Cough, Sidney Evans, Dan Davies, and I sat on the roof of a lorry travelling to the end of the Peninsula. It was a tall, six-wheeled lorry, from which we could spit on the roofs of the passing cars and throw our apple stumps at women on the pavement. One stump caught a man on a bicycle in the middle of the back, he swerved across the road, for a moment we sat quiet and George Hooping's face grew pale. And if the lorry runs over him, I thought calmly as the man on the bicycle swayed towards the hedge, he'll get killed and I'll be sick on my trousers and perhaps on Sidney's too, and we'll all be arrested and hanged, except George Hooping who didn't have an apple.

But the lorry swept past; behind us, the bicycle drove into the hedge, the man stood up and waved his fist, and I waved my cap back at him.

'You shouldn't have waved your cap,' said Sidney Evans, 'he'll know what school we're in.' He was clever, dark, and careful, and had a purse and a wallet.

'We're not in school now.'

'Nobody can expel me,' said Dan Davies. He was leaving next term to serve in his father's fruit shop for a salary.

We all wore haversacks, except George Hooping whose mother had given him a brown-paper parcel that kept coming undone, and carried a suitcase each. I had placed a coat over my suitcase because the initials on it were 'N. T.' and everybody would know that it belonged to my sister. Inside the lorry were two tents, a box of food, a packing-case of kettles and saucepans and knives and forks, an oil lamp, a primus stove, ground sheets and blankets, a gramophone with three records, and a table-cloth from George Hooping's mother.

We were going to camp for a fortnight in Rhossilli, in a field above the sweeping five-mile beach. Sidney and Dan had stayed there last year, coming back brown and swearing, full of stories of campers' dances round the fires at midnight, and elderly girls from the training college who sun-bathed naked on ledges of rocks surrounded by laughing boys, and singing in bed that lasted until dawn. But George had never left home for more than a night; and then, he told me one half-holiday when it was raining and there was nothing to do but to stay in the washhouse racing his guinea-pigs giddily along the benches, it was only to stay in St Thomas, three miles from his house, with an aunt who could see through the walls and who knew what a Mrs Hoskin was doing in the kitchen.

'How much further?' asked George Hooping, clinging to his split parcel, trying in secret to push back socks and suspenders, enviously watching the solid green fields skim by as though the roof were a raft on an ocean with a motor in it. Anything upset his stomach, even liquorice and sherbet, but I alone knew that he wore long combinations in the summer with his name stitched in red on them.

'Miles and miles,' Dan sad.

'Thousands of miles,' I said. 'It's Rhossilli, U.S.A. We're going to camp on a bit of rock that wobbles in the wind.'

'And we have to tie the rock on to a tree.'

'Cough can use his suspenders,' Sidney said.

The lorry roared round a corner—'Upsy-daisy! Did you feel it then, Cough? It was on one wheel'—and below us, beyond fields and farms, the sea, with a steamer puffing on its far edge, shimmered.

'Do you see the sea down there, it's shimmering, Dan,' I said.

George Hooping pretended to forget the lurch of the slippery roof and, from that height, the frightening smallness of the sea. Gripping the rail of the roof, he said: 'My father saw a killer whale.' The conviction in his voice died quickly as he began. He beat against the wind with his cracked, treble voice, trying to make us believe. I knew he wanted to find a boast so big it would make our hair stand up and stop the wild lorry.

'Your father's a herbalist.' But the smoke on the horizon was the white, curling fountain the whale blew through his nose, and its black nose was the bow of the poking ship.

'Where did he keep it, Cough, in the washhouse?'

'He saw it in Madagascar. It had tusks as long as from here to, from here to . . .'

'From here to Madagascar.'

All at once the threat of a steep hill disturbed him. No longer bothered about the adventures of his father, a small, dusty, skull-capped and alpaca-coated man standing and mumbling all day in a shop full of herbs and curtained holes in the wall, where old men with backache and young girls in trouble waited for consultations in the half-dark, he stared at the hill swooping up and clung to Dan and me.

'She's doing fifty!'

'The brakes have gone, Cough!'

He twisted away from us, caught hard with both hands on the rail, pulled and trembled, pressed on a case behind him with his foot, and steered the lorry to safety round a stone-walled corner and up a gentler hill to the gate of a battered farm-house.

Leading down from the gate, there was a lane to the first beach. It was high tide, and we heard the sea dashing. Four boys on a roof—one tall, dark, regular-featured, precise of speech, in a good suit, a boy of the world; one squat, ungainly, red-haired, his red wrists fighting out of short, frayed sleeves; one heavily spectacled, small-paunched, with indoor shoulders and feet in always unlaced boots wanting to go different ways; one small, thin, indecisively active, quick to get dirty, curly—saw their field in front of them, a fortnight's new home that had thick, pricking hedges for walls, the sea for a front garden, a green gutter for a lavatory, and a wind-struck tree in the very middle.

I helped Dan unload the lorry while Sidney tipped the driver and George struggled with the farm-yard gate and looked at the ducks inside. The lorry drove away.

'Let's build our tents by the tree in the middle,' said George.

'Pitch!' Sidney said, unlatching the gate for him.

We pitched our tents in a corner, out of the wind.

'One of us must light the primus,' Sidney said, and, after George had burned his hand, we sat in a circle outside the sleeping-tent talking about motor cars, content to be in the country, lazily easy in each other's company, thinking to ourselves as we talked, knowing always that the sea dashed on the rocks not far below us and rolled out into the world, and that to-morrow we would bathe and throw a ball on the sands and stone a bottle on a rock and perhaps meet three girls. The oldest would be for Sidney, the plainest for Dan, and the youngest for me. George broke his spectacles when he spoke to girls; he had to walk off, blind as a bat, and the next morning he would say: 'I'm sorry I had to leave you, but I remembered a message.'

It was past five o'clock. My father and mother would have finished tea; the plates with famous castles on them were cleared from the table; father with a newspaper, mother with socks, were far away in the blue haze to the left, up a hill, in a villa, hearing from the park the faint cries of children drift over the public tennis court, and wondering where I was and what I was doing. I was alone with my friends in a field, with a blade of grass in my mouth, saying, 'Dempsey would hit him cold,' and thinking of the great whale that George's father never saw thrashing on the top of the sea, or plunging underneath, like a mountain.

'Bet you I can beat you to the end of the field.'

Dan and I raced among the cowpads, George thumping at our heels.

'Let's go down to the beach.'

Sidney led the way, running straight as a soldier in his khaki shorts, over a stile, down fields to another, into a wooded valley, up through heather on to a clearing near the edge of the cliff, where two broad boys were wrestling outside a tent. I saw one bite the other in the leg, they both struck expertly and savagely at the face, one struggled clear, and, with a leap, the other had him face to the ground. They were Brazell and Skully.

'Hallo, Brazell and Skully!' said Dan.

Skully had Brazell's arm in a policeman's grip; he gave it two quick twists and stood up, smiling.

'Hallo, boys! Hallo, Little Cough! How's your father?'

'He's very well, thank you.'

Brazell, on the grass, felt for broken bones. 'Hallo, boys! How are your fathers?'

They were the worst and biggest boys in school. Every day for a term they caught me before class began and wedged me in the wastepaper basket and then put the basket on the master's desk. Sometimes I could get out and sometimes not. Brazell was lean, Skully was fat.

'We're camping in Button's field,' said Sidney.

'We're taking a rest cure here,' said Brazell. 'And how is Little Cough these days? Father given him a pill?'

We wanted to run down to the beach, Dan and Sidney and George and I, to be alone together, to walk and shout by the sea in the country, throw stones at the waves, remember adventures and make more to remember.

'We'll come down to the beach with you,' said Skully.

He linked arms with Brazell, and they strolled behind us, imitating George's wayward walk and slashing the grass with switches.

Dan said hopefully: 'Are you camping here for long, Brazell and Skully?'

'For a whole nice fortnight, Davies and Thomas and Evans and Hooping.'

When we reached Mewslade beach and flung ourselves down, as I scooped up sand and let it trickle grain by grain through my fingers, as George peered at the sea through his double lenses and Sidney and Dan heaped sand over his legs, Brazell and Skully sat behind us like two warders.

'We thought of going to Nice for a fortnight,' said Brazell—he rhymed it with ice, dug Skully in the ribs—'but the air's nicer here for the complexion.'

'It's as good as a herb,' said Skully.

They shared an enormous joke, cuffing and biting and wrestling again, scattering sand in the eyes, until they fell back with laughter, and Brazell wiped the blood from his nose with a piece of picnic paper. George lay covered to the waist in sand. I watched the sea slipping out, with birds quarrelling over it, and the sun beginning to go down patiently.

'Look at Little Cough,' said Brazell. 'Isn't he extraordinary? He's growing out of the sand. Little Cough hasn't got any legs.'

'Poor Little Cough,' said Skully, 'he's the most extraordinary boy in the world.'

'Extraordinary Little Cough,' they said together, 'extraordinary, extraordinary, extraordinary.' They made a song out of it, and both conducted with their switches.

'He can't swim.'

'He can't run.'

'He can't learn.'

'He can't bowl.'

'He can't bat.'

'And I bet he can't make water.'

George kicked the sand from his legs. 'Yes, I can!'

'Can you swim?'

'Can you run?'

'Can you bowl?'

'Leave him alone,' Dan said.

They shuffled nearer to us. The sea was racing out now. Brazell said in a serious voice, wagging his finger: 'Now, quite truthfully, Cough, aren't you extraordinary? Very extraordinary? Say "Yes" or "No."'

'Categorically, "Yes" or "No,"' said Skully.

'No,' George said. 'I can swim and I can run and I can play cricket. I'm not frightened of anybody.'

I said: 'He was second in the form last term.'

'Now isn't that extraordinary? If he can be second he can be first. But no, that's too ordinary. Little Cough must be second.'

'The question is answered,' said Skully. 'Little Cough is extraordinary.' They began to sing again.

'He's a very good runner,' Dan said.

'Well, let him prove it. Skully and I ran the whole length of Rhossilli sands this morning, didn't we, Skull?'

'Every inch.'

'Can Little Cough do it?'

'Yes,' said George.

'Do it, then.'

'I don't want to.'

'Extraordinary Little Cough can't run,' they sang, 'can't run, can't run.'

Three girls, all fair, came down the cliffside arm in arm, dressed in short, white trousers. Their arms and legs and throats were brown as berries; I could see when they laughed that their teeth were very white; they stepped on to the beach, and Brazell and Skully stopped singing. Sidney smoothed his hair back, rose casually, put his hands in his pockets, and walked towards the girls, who now stood close together, gold and brown, admiring the sunset with little attention, patting their scarves, turning smiles on each other. He stood in front of them, grinned, and saluted: 'Hallo, Gwyneth! do you remember me?'

'La-di-da!' whispered Dan at my side, and made a mock salute to George still peering at the retreating sea.

'Well, if this isn't a surprise!' said the tallest girl. With little studied movements of her hands, as though she were distributing flowers, she introduced Peggy and Jean.

Fat Peggy, I thought, too jolly for me, with hockey legs and tomboy crop, was the girl for Dan; Sidney's Gwyneth was a distinguished piece and quite sixteen, as immaculate and unapproachable as a girl in Ben Evans' stores; but Jean, shy and curly, with butter-coloured hair, was mine. Dan and I walked slowly to the girls.

I made up two remarks: 'Fair's fair, Sidney, no bigamy abroad,' and 'Sorry we couldn't arrange to have the sea in when you came.'

Jean smiled, wriggling her heel in the sand, and I raised my cap.

'Hallo!'

The cap dropped at her feet.

As I bent down, three lumps of sugar fell from my blazer pocket. 'I've been feeding a horse,' I said, and began to blush guiltily when all the girls laughed.

I could have swept the ground with my cap, kissed my hand gaily, called them señoritas, and made them smile without tolerance. Or I could have stayed at a distance, and this would have been better still, my hair blown in the wind, though there was no wind at all that evening, wrapped in mystery and staring at the sun, too aloof to speak to girls; but I knew that all the time my ears would have been burning, my stomach would have been as hollow and as full of voices as a shell. 'Speak to them quickly, before they go away!' a voice would have said insistently over the dramatic silence, as I stood like Valentino on the edge of the bright, invisible bull-ring of the sands. 'Isn't it lovely here!' I said.

I spoke to Jean alone; and this is love, I thought, as she nodded her head and swung her curls and said: 'It's nicer than Porthcawl.'

Brazell and Skully were two big bullies in a nightmare; I forgot them when Jean and I walked up the cliff, and, looking back to see if they were baiting George again or wrestling together, I saw that George had disappeared around the corner of the rocks and that they were talking at the foot of the with Sidney and the two girls.

'What's your name?'

I told her.

'That's Welsh,' she said.

'You've got a beautiful name.'

'Oh! it's just ordinary.'

'Shall I see you again?'

'If you want to.'

'I want to all right! We can go and bathe in the morning. And we can try to get an eagle's egg. Did you know that there were eagles here?'

'No,' she said. 'Who was that handsome boy on the beach, the tall one with dirty trousers?'

'He's not handsome, that's Brazell. He never washes or combs his hair or anything. And he's a bully and he cheats.'

'I think he's handsome.'

We walked into Button's field, and I showed her inside the tents and gave her one of George's apples. 'I'd like a cigarette,' she said.

It was nearly dark when the others came. Brazell and Skully were with Gwyneth, one each side of her holding her arms, Sidney was with Peggy, and Dan walked, whistling, behind with his hands in his pockets.

'There's a pair,' said Brazell, 'they've been here all alone and they aren't even holding hands. You want a pill,' he said to me.

'Build Britain's babies,' said Skully.

'Go on!' Gwyneth said. She pushed him away from her, but she was laughing, and she said nothing when he put his arm around her waist.

'What about a bit of fire?' said Brazell.

Jean clapped her hands like an actress. Although I knew I loved her, I didn't like anything she said or did.

'Who's going to make it?'

'He's the best, I'm sure,' she said, pointing to me.

Dan and I collected sticks, and by the time it was quite dark there was a fire crackling. Inside the sleeping-tent, Brazell and Jean sat close together; her golden head was on his shoulder; Skully, near them, whispered to Gwyneth; Sidney unhappily held Peggy's hand.

'Did you ever see such a sloppy lot?' I said, watching Jean smile in the fiery dark.

'Kiss me, Charley!' said Dan.

We sat by the fire in the corner of the field. The sea, far out, was still making a noise. We heard a few nightbirds. '"Tu-whit! tu-whoo!" Listen! I don't like owls,' Dan said, 'they scratch your eyes out!'—and tried not to listen to the soft voices in the tent. Gwyneth's laughter floated out over the suddenly moonlit field, but Jean, with the beast, was smiling and silent in the covered warmth; I knew her little hand was in Brazell's hand.

'Women!' I said.

Dan spat in the fire.

We were old and alone, sitting beyond desire in the middle of the night, when George appeared, like a ghost, in the firelight and stood there trembling until I said: 'Where've you been? You've been gone hours. Why are you trembling like that?'

Brazell and Skully poked their heads out.

'Hallo, Cough my boy! How's your father? What have you been up to to-night?'

George Hooping could hardly stand. I put my hand on his shoulder to steady him, but he pushed it away.

'I've been running on Rhossilli sands! I ran every bit of it! You said I couldn't, and I did! I've been running and running!'

Someone inside the tent put a record on the gramophone. It was a selection from *No, No, Nanette*.

'You've been running all the time in the dark, Little Cough?'

'And I bet I ran it quicker than you did, too!' George said.

'I bet you did,' said Brazell.

'Do you think we'd run five miles?' said Skully.

Now the tune was 'Tea for Two.'

'Did you ever hear anything so extraordinary? I told you Cough was extraordinary. Little Cough's been running all night.'

'Extraordinary, extraordinary, extraordinary Little Cough,' they said.

Laughing from the shelter of the tent into the darkness, they looked like a boy with two heads. And when I stared round at George again he was lying on his back fast asleep in the deep grass and his hair was touching the flames.

Just Like Little Dogs

Standing alone under a railway arch out of the wind, I was looking at the miles of sands, long and dirty in the early dark, with only a few boys on the edge of the sea and one or two hurrying couples with their mackintoshes blown around them like balloons, when two young men joined me, it seemed out of nowhere, and struck matches for their cigarettes and illuminated their faces under bright-checked caps.

One had a pleasant face; his eyebrows slanted comically towards his temples, his eyes were warm, brown, deep, and guileless, and his mouth was full and weak. The other man had a boxer's nose and a weighted chin ginger with bristles.

We watched the boys returning from the oily sea; they shouted under the echoing arch, then their voices faded. Soon there was not a couple in sight; the lovers had disappeared among the sandhills and were lying down there with the broken tins and bottles of the summer passed, old paper blowing by them, and nobody with any sense was about. The strangers, huddled against the wall, their hands deep in their pockets, their cigarettes sparkling, stared, I thought, at the thickening of the dark over the empty sands, but their eyes may have been closed. A train raced over us, and the arch shook. Over the shore, behind the vanishing train, smoke clouds flew together, rags of wings and hollow bodies of great birds black as tunnels, and broke up lazily; cinders fell through a sieve in the air, and the sparks were put out by the wet dark before they reached the sand. The night before, little quick scarecrows had bent and picked at the track-line and a solitary dignified scavenger wandered three miles by the edge with a crumpled coal sack and a park-keeper's steel-tipped stick. Now they were tucked up in sacks, asleep in a siding, their heads in bins, their beards in straw, in coal-trucks thinking of fires, or lying beyond pickings on Jack Stiff's slab near the pub in the Fishguard Alley, where the methylated-spirit drinkers danced into the policemen's arms and women like lumps of clothes in a pool waited, in doorways and holes in the soaking wall, for vampires or firemen. Night was properly down on us now. The wind changed. Thin rain began. The sands themselves went out. We stood in the scooped, windy room of the arch, listening to the noises from the muffled town, a goods train shunting, a siren in the docks, the hoarse trams in the streets far behind, one bark of a dog, unplaceable sounds, iron being beaten, the distant creaking of wood, doors slamming where there were no houses, an engine coughing like a sheep on a hill.

The two young men were statues smoking, tough-capped and collarless watchers and witnesses carved out of the stone of the blowing room where they stood at my side with nowhere to go, nothing to do, and all the raining, almost winter, night before them. I cupped a match to let them see my face in a dramatic shadow, my eyes mysteriously sunk, perhaps, in a startling white face, my young looks savage in the sudden flicker of light, to make them wonder who I was as I puffed my last butt and puzzled about them. Why was the soft-faced young man, with his tame devil's eyebrows, standing like a stone figure with a glowworm in it? He should have a nice girl to bully him gently and take him to cry in the pictures, or kids to bounce in a kitchen in Rodney Street. There was no sense in standing silent for hours under a railway arch on a hell of a night at the end of a bad summer when girls were waiting, ready to be hot and friendly, in chip shops and shop doorways and Rabbiotti's all-night café, when the public bar of the 'Bay View' at the corner had a fire and skittles and a swarthy, sensuous girl with different coloured eyes, when the billiard saloons were open, except the one in High Street you couldn't go into without a collar and tie, when the closed parks had empty, covered bandstands and the railings were easy to climb.

A church clock somewhere struck a lot, faintly from the night on the right, but I didn't count.

The other young man, less than two feet from me, should be shouting with the boys, boasting in lanes, propping counters, prancing and clouting in the Mannesmann Hall, or whispering around a bucket in a ring corner. Why was he humped here with a moody man and myself, listening to our breathing, to the sea, the wind scattering sand through the archway, a chained dog and a foghorn and the rumble of trams a dozen streets away, watching a match strike, a boy's fresh face spying in a shadow, the lighthouse beams, the movement of a hand to a fag, when the sprawling town in a drizzle, the pubs and the clubs and the coffee-shops, the prowlers' streets, the arches near the promenade, were full of friends and enemies? He could be playing nap by a candle in a shed in a wood-yard.

Families sat down to supper in rows of short houses, the wireless sets were on, the daughters' young men sat in the front rooms. In neighbouring houses they read the news off the table-cloth, and the potatoes from dinner were fried up. Cards were played in the front rooms of houses on the hills. In the houses on tops of the hills families were entertaining friends, and the blinds of the front rooms were not quite drawn. I heard the sea in a cold bit of the cheery night.

One of the strangers said suddenly, in a high, clear voice: 'What are we all doing then?'

'Standing under a bloody arch,' said the other one.

'And it's cold,' I said.

'It isn't very cosy,' said the high voice of the young man with the pleasant face, now invisible. 'I've been in better hotels than this.'

'What about that night in the Majestic?' said the other voice.

There was a long silence.

'Do you often stand here?' said the pleasant man. His voice might never have broken.

'No, this is the first time here,' I said. 'Sometimes I stand in the Brynmill arch.'

'Ever tried the old pier?'

'It's no good in the rain, is it?'

'Underneath the pier, I mean, in the girders.'

'No, I haven't been there.'

'Tom spends every Sunday under the pier,' the pug-faced young man said bitterly. 'I got to take him his dinner in a piece of paper.'

'There's another train coming,' I said. It tore over us, the arch bellowed, the wheels screamed through our heads, we were deafened and spark-blinded and crushed under the fiery weight and we rose again, like battered black men, in the grave of the arch. No noise at all from the swallowed town. The trams had rattled themselves dumb. A pressure of the hidden sea rubbed away the smudge of the docks. Only three young men were alive.

One said: 'It's a sad life, without a home.'

'Haven't you got a home then?' I said.

'Oh, yes, I've got a home all right.'

'I got one, too.'

'And I live near Cwmdonkin Park,' I said.

'That's another place Tom sits in in the dark. He says he listens to the owls.'

'I knew a chap once who lived in the country, near Bridgend,' said Tom, 'and they had a munition works there in the War and it spoiled all the birds. The chap I know says you can always tell a cuckoo from Bridgend, it goes: "Cuckbloodyoo! cuckbloodyoo!"'

'Cuckbloodyoo!' echoed the arch.

'Why are you standing under the arch then?' asked Tom. 'It's warm at home. You can draw the curtains and sit by the fire, snug as a bug. Gracie's on the wireless to-night. No shananacking in the old moonlight.'

'I don't want to be home, I don't want to sit by the fire. I've got nothing to do when I'm in and I don't want to go to bed. I like standing about like this with nothing to do, in the dark all by myself,' I said.

And I did, too. I was a lonely night-walker and a steady stander-at-corners. I liked to walk through the wet town after midnight, when the streets were deserted and the window lights out, alone and alive on the glistening tram-lines in dead and empty High Street under the moon, gigantically sad in the damp streets by ghostly Ebenezer Chapel. And I never felt more a part of the remote and overpressing world, or more full of love and arrogance and pity and humility, not for myself alone, but for the living earth I suffered on and for the unfeeling systems in the upper air, Mars and Venus and Brazell and Skully, men in China and St Thomas, scorning girls and ready girls, soldiers and bullies and policemen and sharp, suspicious buyers of second-hand books, bad, ragged women who'd pretend against the museum wall for a cup of tea, and perfect, unapproachable women out of the fashion magazines, seven feet high, sailing slowly in their flat, glazed creations through steel and glass and velvet. I leant against the wall of a derelict house in the residential areas or wandered in the empty rooms, stood terrified on the stairs or gazing through the smashed windows at the sea or at nothing, and the lights going out one by one in the avenues. Or I mooched in a half-built house, with the sky stuck in the roof and cats on the ladders and a wind shaking through the bare bones of the bedrooms.

'And you can talk,' I said. 'Why aren't you at home?'

'I don't want to be home,' said Tom.

'I'm not particular,' said his friend.

When a match flared, their heads rocked and spread on the wall, and shapes of winged bulls and buckets grew bigger and smaller. Tom began to tell a story. I thought of a new stranger walking on the sands past the arch and hearing all of a sudden that high voice out of a hole.

I missed the beginning of the story as I thought of the man on the sands listening in a panic or dodging, like a footballer, in and out among the jumping dark towards the lights behind the railway line, and remembered Tom's voice in the middle of a sentence.

'... went up to them and said it was a lovely night. It wasn't a lovely night at all. The sands were empty. We asked them what their names were and they asked us what ours were. We were walking along by this time. Walter here was telling them about the glee party in the "Melba" and what went on in the ladies' cloakroom. You had to drag the tenors away like ferrets.'

'What were their names?' I asked.

'Doris and Norma,' Walter said.

'So we walked along the sands towards the dunes,' Tom said, 'and Walter was with Doris and I was with Norma. Norma worked in the steam laundry. We hadn't been walking and talking for more than a few minutes when, by God, I knew I was head over heels in love with the girl, and she wasn't the pretty one, either.'

He described her. I saw her clearly. Her plump, kind face, jolly brown eyes, warm wide mouth, thick bobbed hair, rough body, bottle legs, broad bum, grew from a few words right out of Tom's story, and I saw her ambling solidly along the sands in a spotted frock in a showering autumn evening with fancy gloves on her hard hands, a gold bangle, with a voile handkerchief tucked in it, round her wrist, and a navy-blue handbag with letters and outing snaps, a compact, a bus ticket, and a shilling.

'Doris was the pretty one,' said Tom, 'smart and touched up and sharp as a knife. I was twenty-six years old and I'd never been in love, and there I was, gawking at Norma in the middle of Tawe sands, too frightened to put my finger on her gloves. Walter had his arm round Doris then.'

They sheltered behind a dune. The night dropped down on them quickly. Walter was a caution with Doris, hugging and larking, and Tom sat close to Norma, brave enough to hold her hand in its cold glove and tell her all his secrets. He told her his age and his job. He liked staying in in the evenings with a good book. Norma liked dances. He liked dances, too. Norma and Doris were sisters. 'I'd never have thought that,' Tom said, 'you're beautiful, I love you.'

Now the story-telling night in the arch gave place to the loving night in the dunes. The arch was as high as the sky. The faint town noises died. I lay like a pimp in a bush by Tom's side and squinted through to see him round his hands on Norma's breast. 'Don't you dare!' Walter and Doris lay quietly near them. You could have heard a safety-pin fall.

'And the curious thing was,' said Tom, 'that after a time we all sat up on the sand and smiled at each other. And then we all moved softly about on the sand in the dark, without saying a word. And Doris was lying with me, and Norma was with Walter.'

'But why did you change over, if you loved her?' I asked.

'I never understood why,' said Tom. 'I think about it every night.'

'That was in October,' Walter said.

And Tom continued: 'We didn't see much of the girls until July. I couldn't face Norma. Then they brought two paternity orders against us, and Mr Lewis, the magistrate, was eighty years old, and stone deaf, too. He put a little trumpet by his ear and Norma and Doris gave evidence. Then we gave evidence, and he couldn't decide whose was which. And at the end he shook his head back and fore and pointed his trumpet and said: "Just like little dogs!"'

All at once I remembered how cold it was. I rubbed my numb hands together. Fancy standing all night in the cold. Fancy listening, I thought, to a long, unsatisfactory story in the frost-bite night in a polar arch. 'What happened then?' I asked.

Walter answered. 'I married Norma,' he said 'and Tom married Doris. We had to do the right thing by them, didn't we? That's why Tom won't go home. He never goes home till the early morning. I've got to keep him company. He's my brother.'

It would take me ten minutes to run home. I put up my coat collar and pulled my cap down.

'And the curious thing is,' said Tom, 'that I love Norma and Walter doesn't love Norma or Doris. We've two nice little boys. I call mine Norman.'

We all shook hands.

'See you again,' said Walter.

'I'm always hanging about,' said Tom.

'Abyssinia!'

I walked out of the arch, crossed Trafalgar Terrace, and pelted up the steep streets.

Where Tawe Flows

Mr Humphries, Mr Roberts, and young Mr Thomas knocked on the front door of Mr Emlyn Evans's small villa, 'Lavengro,' punctually at nine o'clock in the evening. They waited, hidden behind a veronica bush, while Mr Evans shuffled in carpet slippers up the passage from the back room and had trouble with the bolts.

Mr Humphries was a school teacher, a tall, fair man with a stammer, who had written an unsuccessful novel.

Mr Roberts, a cheerful, disreputable man of middle age, was a collector for an insurance company; they called him in the trade a body-snatcher, and he was known among his friends as Burke and Hare, the Welsh Nationalist. He had once held a high position in a brewery office.

Young Mr Thomas was at the moment without employment, but it was understood that he would soon be leaving for London to make a career in Chelsea as a free-lance journalist; he was penniless, and hoped, in a vague way, to live on women.

When Mr Evans opened the door and shone his torch down the narrow drive, lighting up the garage and hen-run but missing altogether the whispering bush, the three friends bounded out and cried in threatening voices: 'We're Ogpu men, let us in!'

'We're looking for seditious literature,' said Mr Humphries with difficulty, raising his hand in a salute.

'Heil, Saunders Lewis! and we know where to find it,' said Mr Roberts.

Mr Evans turned off his torch. 'Come in out of the night air, boys, and have a drop of something. It's only parsnip wine,' he added.

They removed their hats and coats, piled them on the end of the banister, spoke softly for fear of waking up the twins, George and Celia, and followed Mr Evans into his den.

'Where's the trouble and strife, Mr Evans?' said Mr Roberts in a cockney accent. He warmed his hands in front of the fire and regarded with a smile of surprise, though he visited the house every Friday, the neat rows of books, the ornate roll-top desk that made the parlour into a study, the shining grandfather clock, the photographs of children staring stiffly at a dickybird, the still, delicious home-made wine, that had such an effect, in an old beer bottle, the sleeping tom on the frayed rug. 'At home with the *bourgeoisie*.'

He was himself a homeless bachelor with a past, much in debt, and nothing gave him more pleasure than to envy his friends their wives and comforts and to speak of them intimately and disparagingly.

'In the kitchen,' said Mr Evans, handing out glasses.

'A woman's only place,' said Mr Roberts heartily, 'with one exception.'

Mr Humphries and Mr Thomas arranged the chairs around the fire, and all four sat down, close and confidential and with full glasses in their hands. None of them spoke for a time. They gave one another sly looks, sipped and sighed, lit the cigarettes that Mr Evans produced from a draughts box, and once Mr Humphries glanced at the grandfather clock and winked and put his finger to his lips. Then, as the visitors grew warm and the wine worked and they forgot the bitter night outside, Mr Evans said, with a little shudder of forbidden delight: 'The wife will be going to bed in half an hour. Then we can start the good work. Have you all got yours with you?'

'And the tools,' said Mr Roberts, smacking his side pocket.

'What's the word until then?' said young Mr Thomas.

Mr Humphries 'winked again. 'Mum!'

'I've been waiting for to-night to come round like I used to wait for Saturdays when I was a boy,' said Mr Evans, 'I got a penny then. And it all went on gob-stoppers and jelly-babies, too.'

He was a traveller in rubber, rubber toys and syringes and bath mats. Sometimes Mr Roberts called him the poor man's friend to make him blush. 'No! no! no!' he would say, 'you can look at my samples, there's nothing like that there.' He was a Socialist.

'I used to buy a packet of Cinderellas with my penny,' said Mr Roberts, 'and smoke them in the slaughter-house. The sweetest little smoke in the world. You don't see them now.'

'Do you remember old Jim, the caretaker, in the slaughter-house?' asked Mr Evans.

'He was after my time; I'm no chicken, like you boys.'

'You're not old, Mr Roberts, think of G.B.S.'

'No clean Shavianism for me, I'm an unrepentant eater of birds and beasts,' said Mr Roberts.

'Do you eat flowers, too?'

'Oh! oh! you literary men, don't you talk above my head now. I'm only a poor old resurrectionist on the knocker.'

'He'd put his hand down in the guts-box and bring you out a rat with its neck broken clean as a match for the price of a glass of beer.'

'And it was beer then.'

'Shop! shop!' Mr Humphries beat on the table with his glass. 'You mustn't waste stories, we'll need them all,' he said. 'Have you got the abattoir anecdote down in your memory book, Mr Thomas?'

'I'll remember it.'

'Don't forget, you can only talk at random now,' said Mr Humphries.

'Okay, Roderick!' Mr Thomas said quickly.

Mr Roberts put his hands over his ears. 'The conversation is getting esoteric,' he said. 'Excuse my French! Mr Evans, have you such a thing as a rook rifle? I want to scare the highbrows off. Did I ever tell you the time I lectured to the John O' London's Society on 'The Utility of Uselessness'? That was a poser. I talked about Jack London all the time, and when they said at the end that it wasn't a lecture about what I said it was going to be, I said, "Well, it was useless lecturing about that, wasn't it?" and they hadn't a word to say. Mrs Dr Davies was in the front row, you remember her? She gave that first lecture on W. J. Locke and got spoonered in the middle. Remember her talking about the 'Bevagged Loveabond,' Mr Humphries?'

'Shop! shop!' said Mr Humphries, groaning, 'keep it until after.'

'More parsnip?'

'It goes down the throat like silk, Mr Evans.'

'Like baby's milk.'

'Say when, Mr Roberts.'

'A word of four syllables denoting a period of time. Thank you! I read that on a matchbox.'

'Why don't they have serials on matchboxes? You'd buy the shop up to see what Daphne did next,' Mr Humphries said.

He stopped and looked round in embarrassment at the faces of his friends. Daphne was the name of the grass widow in Manselton for whom Mr Roberts had lost both his reputation and his position in the brewery. He had been in the habit of delivering bottles to her house, free of charge, and he had bought her a cocktail cabinet and given her a hundred pounds and his mother's rings. In return, she held large parties and never invited him. Only Mr Thomas had noticed the name, and he was saying: 'No, Mr Humphries, on toilet rolls would be best.'

'When I was in London,' Mr Roberts said, 'I stayed with a couple called Armitage in Palmer's Green. He made curtains and blinds. They used to leave each other messages on the toilet paper every single day.'

'If you want to make a Venetian blind,' said Mr Evans, 'stick him in the eye with a hatpin.' He felt, always, a little left out of his evenings at home, and he was waiting for Mrs Evans to come in, disapprovingly, from the kitchen.

'I've often had to use, "Dear Tom, don't forget the Watkinses are coming to tea," or, "To Peggy, from Tom, in remembrance." Mr Armitage was a Mosleyite.'

'Thugs!' said Mr Humphries.

'Seriously, what are we going to do about this uniformication of the individual?' Mr Evans asked. Maud was in the kitchen still; he heard her beating the plates.

'Answering your question with another,' said Mr Roberts, putting one hand on Mr Evans's knee, 'what individuality is there left? The mass-age produces the mass-man. The machine produces the robot.'

'As its slave,' Mr Humphries articulated clearly, 'not, mark you, as its master.'

'There you have it. There it is. Tyrannic dominance by a sparking plug, Mr Humphries, and it's flesh and blood that always pays.'

'Any empty glasses?'

Mr Roberts turned his glass upside down. 'That used to mean, "I'll take on the best man in the room in a bout of fisticuffs," in Llanelly. But seriously, as Mr Evans says, the old-fashioned individualist is a square peg now in a round hole.'

'What a hole!' said Mr Thomas.

'Take our national—what did Onlooker say last week?—our national misleaders.'

'You take them, Mr Roberts, we've got rats already,' Mr Evans said with a nervous laugh. The kitchen was silent. Maud was ready.

'Onlooker is a *nom de plume* for Basil Gorse-Williams,' said Mr Humphries. 'Did any one know that?'

'*Nom de guerre.* Did you see his article on Ramsay Mac? "A sheep in wolf's clothing."'

'Know him!' Mr Roberts said scornfully, 'I've been sick on him.'

Mrs Evans heard the last remark as she came into the room. She was a thin woman with bitter lines, tired hands, the ruins of fine brown eyes, and a superior nose. An unshockable woman, she had once listened to Mr Roberts's description of his haemorrhoids for over an hour on a New Year's Eve and had allowed him, without protest, to call them the grapes of wrath. When sober, Mr Roberts addressed her as 'ma'am' and kept the talk to weather and colds. He sprang to his feet and offered her his chair.

'No, thank you, Mr Roberts,' she said in a clear, hard voice, 'I'm going to bed at once. The cold disagrees with me.'

Go to bed, plain Maud, thought young Mr Thomas. 'Will you have a little warm, Mrs Evans, before you retire?' he said.

She shook her head, gave the friends a thin smile, and said to Mr Evans: 'Put the world right before you come to bed.'

'Good night, Mrs Evans.'

'It won't be after midnight this time, Maud, I promise. I'll put Sambo out in the back.'

'Good night, ma'am.'

Sleep tight, hoity.

'I won't disturb you gentlemen any more,' she said. 'What's left of the parsnip wine for Christmas is in the boot cupboard, Emlyn. Don't let it waste. Good night.'

Mr Evans raised his eyebrows and whistled. 'Whew! boys.' He pretended to fan his face with his tie. Then his hand stopped still in the air. 'She was used to a big house,' he said, 'with servants.'

Mr Roberts brought out pencils and fountain pens from his side pocket. 'Where's the priceless MS.? Tempus is fugiting.'

Mr Humphries and Mr Thomas put notebooks on their knees, took a pencil each, and watched Mr Evans open the door of the grandfather clock. Beneath the swinging weights was a heap of papers tied up in a blue bow. These Mr Evans placed on the desk.

'I call order,' said Mr Roberts. 'Let's see where we were. Have you got the minutes, Mr Thomas?'

"'*Where Tawe flows*,'" said Mr Thomas, "'a Novel of Provincial Life. Chapter One: a cross-section description of the town, Dockland, Slums, Suburbia, etc." We finished that. The title decided upon was: Chapter One, "The Public Town." Chapter Two is to be called "The Private Lives," and Mr Humphries has proposed the following: "Each of the collaborators take one character from each social sphere or stratum of the town and introduce him to the readers with a brief history of his life up to the point at which we commence the story, i.e. the winter of this very year. These introductions of the characters, hereafter to be regarded as the principal protagonists, and their biographical chronicles, shall constitute the second chapter." Any questions, gentlemen?'

Mr Humphries agreed with all he had said. His character was a sensitive schoolmaster of advanced opinions, who was misjudged and badly treated.

'No questions,' said Mr Evan's. He was in charge of Suburbia. He rustled his notes and waited to begin.

'I haven't written anything yet,' Mr Roberts said, 'it's all in my head.' He had chosen the Slums.

'Personally,' said Mr Thomas, 'I haven't made up my mind whether to have a barmaid or a harlot.'

'What about a barmaid who's a harlot too?' Mr Roberts suggested. 'Or perhaps we could have a couple of characters each? I'd like to do an alderman. And a gold-digger.'

'Who had a word for them, Mr Humphries?' said Mr Thomas.

'The Greeks.'

Mr Roberts nudged Mr Evans and whispered: 'I just thought of an opening sentence for my bit. Listen, Emlyn. "On the rickety table in the corner of the crowded, dilapidated room, a stranger might have seen, by the light of the flickering candle in the gin-bottle, a broken cup, full of sick or custard."'

'Be serious, Ted,' said Mr Evans, laughing. 'You wrote that sentence down.'

'No, I swear, it came to me just like that!' He flicked his fingers. 'And who's been reading my notes?'

'Have you put anything on paper yourself, Mr Thomas?'

'Not yet, Mr Evans.' He had been writing, that week, the story of a cat who jumped over a woman the moment she died and turned her into a vampire. He had reached the part of the story where the woman was an undead children's governess, but he could not think how to fit it into the novel.

'There's no need, is there,' he asked, 'for us to avoid the fantastic altogether?'

'Wait a bit! wait a bit!' said Mr Humphries, 'let's get our realism straight. Mr Thomas will be making all the characters Blue Birds before we know where we are. One thing at a time. Has any one got the history of his character ready?' He had his biography in his hand, written in red ink. The writing was scholarly and neat and small.

'I think my character is ready to take the stage,' said Mr Evans. 'But I haven't written it out. I'll have to refer to the notes and make the rest up out of my head. It's a very silly story.'

'Well, you must begin, of course,' said Mr Humphries with disappointment.

'Everybody's biography is silly,' Mr Roberts said. 'My own would make a cat laugh.'

Mr Humphries said: 'I must disagree there. The life of that mythical common denominator, the man in the street, is dull as ditch-water, Mr Roberts. Capitalist society has made him a mere bundle of repressions and useless habits under that symbol of middle-class divinity, the bowler.' He looked quickly away from the notes in the palm of his hand. 'The ceaseless toil for bread and butter, the ogres of unemployment, the pettifogging gods of gentility, the hollow lies of the marriage bed. Marriage,' he said, dropping his ash on the carpet, 'legal monogamous prostitution.'

'Whoa! whoa! there he goes!'

'Mr Humphries is on his hobby-horse again.'

'I'm afraid,' said Mr Evans, 'that I lack our friend's extensive vocabulary. Have pity on a poor amateur. You're shaming my little story before I begin.'

'I still think the life of the ordinary man is most extraordinary,' Mr Roberts said, 'take my own . . .'

'As the secretary,' said Mr Thomas, 'I vote we take Mr Evans's story. We must try to get *Tawe* finished for the spring list.'

'My *To-morrow and To-morrow* was published in the summer in a heat wave,' Mr Humphries said.

Mr Evans coughed, looked into the fire, and began.

'Her name is Mary,' he said, 'but that's not her name really. I'm calling her that because she is a real woman and we don't want any libel. She lives in a house called "Bellevue," but that's not the proper name, of course. A villa by any other name, Mr Humphries. I chose her for my character because her life story is a little tragedy, but it's not without its touches of humour either. It's almost Russian. Mary—Mary Morgan now but she was Mary Phillips before she married and that comes later, that's the anti-climax—wasn't a suburbanite from birth, she didn't live under the shadow of the bowler, like you and me. Or like me, anyway. I was born in "The Poplars" and now I'm in "Lavengro." From bowler to bowler, though I must say, apropos of Mr Humphries's diatribe, and I'm the first to admire his point of view, that the everyday man's just as interesting a character study as the neurotic poets of Bloomsbury.'

'Remind me to shake your hand,' said Mr Roberts.

'You've been reading the Sunday papers,' said Mr Humphries accusingly.

'You two argue the toss later on,' Mr Thomas said. "Is the Ordinary Man a Mouse?" Now, what about Mary?'

'Mary Phillips,' continued Mr Evans, '—and any more interruptions from the intelligentsia and I'll get Mr Roberts to tell you the story of his operations, no pardons granted—lived on a big farm in Carmarthenshire, I'm not going to tell you exactly where, and her father was a widower. He had any amount of what counts and he drank like a fish, but he was always a gentleman with it. Now, now! forget the class war, I could see it smouldering. He came of a very good, solid family, but he raised his elbow, that's all there is to it.'

Mr Roberts said: 'Huntin', fishin', and boozin'."

'No, he wasn't quite county and he wasn't a *nouveau riche* either. No Philippstein about him, though I'm not an anti-Semite. You've only got to think of Einstein and Freud. There are bad Christians, too. He was just what I'm telling you, if you'd only let me, a man of good old farming stock who'd made his pile and now he was spending it.'

'Liquidating it.'

'He'd only got one child, and that was Mary, and she was so prim and proper she couldn't bear to see him the worse for drink. Every night he came home, and he was always the worse, she'd shut herself in her bedroom and hear him rolling about the house and calling for her and breaking the china sometimes. But only sometimes, and he wouldn't have hurt a hair of her head. She was about eighteen and a fine-looking girl, not a film star, mind, not Mr Roberts's type at all, and perhaps she had an Oedipus complex, but she hated her father and she was ashamed of him.'

'What's my type, Mr Evans?'

'Don't pretend not to know, Mr Roberts. Mr Evans means the sort you can take home and show her your stamp collection.'

'I will have hush,' said Mr Thomas.

"'Ave 'ush, is the phrase,' Mr Roberts said. 'Mr Thomas, you're afraid we'll think you're patronizing the lower classes if you drop your aspirates.'

'No nasturtiums, Mr Roberts,' said Mr Humphries.

'Mary Phillips fell in love with a young man whom I shall call Marcus David,' Mr Evans went on, still staring at the fire, avoiding his friends' eyes, and speaking to the burning pictures, 'and she told her father: "Father, Marcus and I want to be engaged. I'm bringing him home one night for supper, and you must promise me that you'll be sober."

'He said, "I'm always sober!" but he wasn't sober when he said it, and after a time he promised.

'"If you break your word, I'll never forgive you," Mary said to him.

'Marcus was a wealthy farmer's son from another district, a bit of a Valentino in a bucolic way, if you can imagine that. She invited him to supper, and he came, very handsome, with larded hair. The servants were out. Mr Phillips had gone to a mart that morning and hadn't returned. She answered the door herself. It was a winter's evening.

'Picture the scene. A prim, well-bred country girl, full of fixations and phobias, proud as a duchess, and blushing like a dairymaid, opening the door to her beloved and seeing him standing there on the pitch-black threshold, shy and handsome. This is from my notes.

'Her future hung on that evening as on a thread. "Come in," she insisted. They didn't kiss, but she wanted him to bow and print his lips on her hand. She took him over the house, which had been specially cleaned and polished, and showed him the case with Swansea china in it. There wasn't a portrait gallery, so she showed him the snaps of her mother in the hall and the photograph of her father, tall and young and sober, in the suit he hunted otters in. And all the time she was proudly parading their possessions, attempting to prove to Marcus, whose father was a J.P., that her background was prosperous enough for her to be his bride, she was waiting fearfully the entrance of her father.

'"O God," she was praying, when they sat down to a cold supper, "that my father will arrive presentable." Call her a snob, if you will, but remember that the life of country gentry, or near gentry, was bound and dictated by the antiquated totems and fetishes of possession. Over supper she told him her family tree and hoped the supper was to his taste. It should have been a hot supper, but she didn't want him to see the servants who were old and dirty. Her father wouldn't change them because they'd always been with him, and there you see the Toryism of this particular society rampant. To cut a long story (this is only the gist, Mr Thomas), they were half-way through supper, and their conversation was becoming more intimate, and she had almost forgotten her father, when the front door burst open and Mr Phillips staggered into the passage, drunk as a judge. The dining-room door was ajar and they could see him plainly. I will not try to describe Mary's kaleidoscopic emotions as her father rocked and mumbled in a thick voice in the passage. He was a big man—I forgot to tell you—six foot and eighteen stone.

"'Quick! quick! under the table!" she whispered urgently, and she pulled Marcus by the hand and they crouched under the table. What bewilderment Marcus experienced we shall never know.

'Mr Phillips came in and saw nobody and sat down at the table and finished all the supper. He licked both plates clean, and under the table they heard him swearing and guzzling. Every time Marcus fidgeted, Mary said: "Shhh!"

'When there was nothing left to eat, Mr Phillips wandered out of the room. They saw his legs. Then, somehow, he climbed upstairs, saying words that made Mary shudder under the table, words of four syllables.'

'Give us three guesses,' said Mr Roberts.

'And she heard him go into his bedroom. She and Marcus crept out of hiding and sat down in front of their empty plates.

"'I don't know how to apologize, Mr David," she said, and she was nearly crying.

"'There's nothing the matter," he said, he was an amenable young man by all accounts, "he's only been to the mart at Carmarthen. I don't like t.t.s myself."

"'Drink makes men sodden beasts," she said.

'He said she had nothing to worry about and that he didn't mind, and she offered him fruit.

"'What will you think of us, Mr David? I've never seen him like that before."

'The little adventure brought them closer together, and soon they were smiling at one another and her wounded pride was almost healed again, but suddenly Mr Phillips opened his bedroom door and charged downstairs, eighteen stone of him, shaking the house.

'"Go away!" she cried softly to Marcus, "please go away before he comes in!"

'There wasn't time. Mr Phillips stood in the passage in the nude.

'She dragged Marcus under the table again, and she covered her eyes not to see her father. She could hear him fumbling in the hallstand for an umbrella, and she knew what he was going to do. He was going outside to obey a call of nature. "O God," she prayed, "let him find an umbrella and go out. Not in the passage! Not in the passage!" They heard him shout for his umbrella. She uncovered her eyes and saw him pulling the front door down. He tore it off its hinges and held it flat above him and tottered out into the dark.

'"Hurry! please hurry!" she said. "Leave me now, Mr David." She drove him out from under the table.

'"Please, please go now," she said, "we'll never meet again. Leave me to my shame." She began to cry, and he ran out of the house. And she stayed under the table all night.'

'Is that all?' said Mr Roberts. 'A very moving incident, Emlyn. How did you come by it?'

'How can it be all?' said Mr Humphries. 'It doesn't explain how Mary Phillips reached "Bellevue." We've left her under a table in Carmarthenshire.'

'I think Marcus is a fellow to be despised,' Mr Thomas said. 'I'd never leave a girl like that, would you, Mr Humphries?'

'Under a table, too. That's the bit I like. That's a position. Perspectives were different,' said Mr Roberts, 'in those days. That narrow puritanism is a spent force. Imagine Mrs Evans under the table. And what happened afterwards? Did the girl die of cramp?'

Mr Evans turned from the fire to reprove him. 'Be as flippant as you will, but the fact remains that an incident like that has a lasting effect on a proud, sensitive girl like Mary. I'm not defending her sensitivity, the whole basis of her pride is outmoded. The social system, Mr Roberts, is not in the box. I'm telling you an incident that occurred. Its social implications are outside our concern.'

'I'm put in my place, Mr Evans.'

'What happened to Mary then?'

'Don't vex him, Mr Thomas, he'll bite your head off.'

Mr Evans went out for more parsnip wine, and, returning, said:

'What happened next? Oh! Mary left her father, of course. She said she'd never forgive him, and she didn't, so she went to live with her uncle in Cardiganshire, a Dr Emyr Lloyd. He was a J.P. too, and rolling in it, about seventy-five—now, remember the age—with a big practice and influential friends. One of his oldest friends was John William Hughes—that's not his name—the London draper, who had a country house near his. Remember what the great Caradoc Evans says? The Cardies always go back to Wales to die when they've rooked the cockneys and made a packet.

'And the only son, Henry William Hughes, who was a nicely educated young man, fell in love with Mary as soon as he saw her and she forgot Marcus and her shame under the table and she fell in love with him. Now don't look disappointed before I begin, this isn't a love story. But they decided to get married, and John William Hughes gave his consent because Mary's uncle was one of the most respected men in the country and her father had money and it would come to her when he died and he was doing his best.

'They were to be married quietly in London. Everything was arranged. Mr Phillips wasn't invited. Mary had her trousseau. Dr Lloyd was to give her away. Beatrice and Betti William Hughes were bridesmaids. Mary went up to London with Beatrice and Betti and stayed with a cousin, and Henry William Hughes stayed in the flat above his father's shop, and the day before the wedding Dr Lloyd arrived from the country, saw Mary for tea, and had dinner with John William Hughes. I wonder who paid for it, too. Then Dr Lloyd retired to his hotel. I'm giving you these trivial details so that you can see how orderly and ordinary everything was. There the actors were, safe and sure.

'Next day, just before the ceremony was to begin, Mary and her cousin, whose name and character are extraneous, and the two sisters, they were both plain and thirty, waited impatiently for Dr Lloyd to call on them. The minutes passed by, Mary was crying, the sisters were sulking, the cousin was getting in everybody's way, but the doctor didn't come. The cousin telephoned the doctor's hotel, but she was told he hadn't spent the night there. Yes, the clerk in the hotel said, he knew the doctor was going to a wedding. No, his bed hadn't been slept in. The clerk suggested that perhaps he was waiting at the church.

'The taxi was ticking away, and that worried Beatrice and Betti, and at last the sisters and the cousin and Mary drove together to the church. A crowd had gathered outside. The cousin poked her head out of the taxi window and asked a policeman to call a churchwarden, and the warden said that Dr Lloyd wasn't there and the groom and the best man were waiting. You can imagine Mary Phillips's feelings when she saw a commotion at the church door and a policeman leading her father out. Mr Phillips had his pockets full of bottles, and how he ever got into the church in the first place no one knew.'

'That's the last straw,' said Mr Roberts.

'Beatrice and Betti said to her: "Don't cry, Mary, the policeman's taking him away. Look! he's fallen in the gutter! There's a splash! Don't take on, it'll be all over soon. You'll be Mrs Henry William Hughes." They were doing their best.

'"You can marry without Dr Lloyd," the cousin told her, and she brightened through her tears—anybody would be crying—and at that moment another policeman——'

'Another!' said Mr Roberts.

'—made his way through the crowd and walked up to the door of the church and sent a message inside. John William Hughes and Henry William Hughes and the best man came out, and they all talked to the policeman, waving their arms and pointing to the taxi with Mary and the bridesmaids and the cousin in it.

'John William Hughes ran down the path to the taxi and shouted through the window: "Dr Lloyd is dead! We'll have to cancel the wedding."

'Henry William Hughes followed him and opened the taxi door and said: "You must drive home, Mary. We've got to go to the police station."

'"And the mortuary," his father said.

'So the taxi drove the bride-to-be home, and the sisters cried worse than she did all the way.'

'That's a sad end,' said Mr Roberts with appreciation. He poured himself another drink.

'It isn't really the end,' Mr Evans said, 'because the wedding wasn't just cancelled. It never came off.'

'But why?' asked Mr Humphries, who had followed the story with a grave expression, even when Mr Phillips fell in the gutter. 'Why should the doctor's death stop everything? She could get someone else to give her away. I'd have done it myself.'

'It wasn't the doctor's death, but where and how he died,' said Mr Evans. 'He died in bed in a bed-sitting-room in the arms of a certain lady. A woman of the town.'

'Kiss me!' Mr Roberts said. 'Seventy-five years old. I'm glad you asked us to remember his age, Mr Evans.'

'But how did Mary Phillips come to live in "Bellevue"? You haven't told us that,' Mr Thomas said.

'The William Hugheses wouldn't have the niece of a man who died in those circumstances——'

'However complimentary to his manhood,' Mr Humphries said, stammering.

'——marry into their family, so she went back to live with her father and he reformed at once—oh! she had a temper, those days—and one day she met a traveller in grain and pigs' food and she married him out of spite. They came to live in "Bellevue," and when Mr Phillips died he left his money to the chapel, so Mary got nothing after all.'

'Nor her husband either. What did you say he travelled in?' asked Mr Roberts.

'Grain and pigs' food.'

After that, Mr Humphries read his biography, which was long and sad and detailed and in good prose; and Mr Roberts told a story about the slums, which could not be included in the book.

Then Mr Evans looked at his watch. 'It's midnight. I promised Maud not after midnight. Where's the cat? I've got to put him out; he tears the cushions. Not that I mind. Sambo! Sambo!'

'There he is, Mr Evans, under the table.'

'Like poor Mary,' said Mr Roberts.

Mr Humphries, Mr Roberts, and young Mr Thomas collected their hats and coats from the banister.

'Do you know what time it is, Emlyn?' Mrs Evans called from upstairs.

Mr Roberts opened the door and hurried out.

'I'm coming now, Maud, I'm just saying good night. Good night,' Mr Evans said in a loud voice. 'Next Friday, nine sharp,' he whispered. 'I'll polish my story up. We'll finish the second chapter and get going on the third. Good night, comrades.'

'Emlyn! Emlyn!' called Mrs Evans.

'Good night, Mary,' said Mr Roberts to the closed door.

The three friends walked down the drive.

Who Do You Wish Was With Us?

Birds in the Crescent trees were singing; boys on bicycles were ringing their bells and pedalling down the slight slope to make the whirrers in their wheels startle the women gabbing on the sunny doorsteps; small girls on the pavement, wheeling young brothers and sisters in prams, were dressed in their summer best and with coloured ribbons; on the circular swing in the public playground, children from the snot school spun themselves happy and sick, crying 'Swing us!' and 'Swing us!' and, 'Ooh! I'm falling!'; the morning was as varied and bright as though it were an international or a jubilee when Raymond Price and I, flannelled and hatless, with sticks and haversacks, set out together to walk to the Worm's Head. Striding along, in step, through the square of the residential Uplands, we brushed by young men in knife-creased whites and showing-off blazers, and hockey-legged girls with towels round their necks and celluloid sun-glasses, and struck a letterbox with our sticks, and bullied our way through a crowd of day-trippers who waited at the stop of the Gower-bound buses, and stepped over luncheon baskets, not caring if we trod in them.

'Why can't those bus lizards walk?' Ray said.

'They were born too tired,' I said.

We went on up Sketty Road at a great speed, our haversacks jumping on our backs. We rapped on every gate to give a terrific walkers' benediction to the people in the choking houses. Like a breath of fresh air we passed a man in office pin-stripes standing, with a dog-lead in his hand, whistling at a corner. Tossing the sounds and smells of the town from us with the swing of our shoulders and loose-limbed strides, halfway up the road we heard women on an outing call 'Mutt and Jeff!' for Ray was tall and thin and I was short. Streamers flew out of the charabanc. Ray, sucking hard at his bulldog pipe, walked too fast to wave and did not even smile. I wondered whom I had missed among the waving women bowling over the rise. My love to come, with a paper cap on, might have sat at the back of the outing, next to the barrel; but, once away from the familiar roads and swinging towards the coast, I forgot her face and voice, that had been made at night, and breathed the country air in.

'There's a different air here. You breathe. It's like the country,' Ray said, 'and a bit of the sea mixed. Draw it down; it'll blow off the nicotine.'

He spat in his hand. 'Still town grey,' he said.

He put back the spit in his mouth and we walked on with our heads high.

By this time we were three miles from the town. The semi-detached houses, with a tin-roofed garage each and a kennel in the back plot and a mowed lawn, with sometimes a hanging coco-nut on a pole, or a birdbath, or a bush like a peacock, grew fewer when we reached the outskirts of the common.

Ray stopped and sighed and said: 'Wait half a sec, I want to fill the old pipe.' He held a match to it as though we were in a storm.

Hot-faced and wet-browed, we grinned at each other. Already the day had brought us close as truants; we were running away, or walking with pride and mischief, arrogantly from the streets that owned us into the unpredictable country. I thought it was against our fate to stride in the sun without the shop-windows dazzling or the music of mowers rising above the birds. A bird's dropping fell on a fence. It was one in the eye for the town. A sheep cried 'Baa!' out of sight, and that would show the Uplands. I did not know what it would show. 'A couple of wanderers in wild Wales,' Ray said, winking, and a lorry carrying cement drove past us towards the golf links. He slapped my haversack and straightened his shoulders. 'Come on, let's be going.' We walked uphill faster than before.

A party of cyclists had pulled up on the roadside and were drinking dandelion and burdock from paper cups. I saw the empty bottles in a bush. All the boys wore singlets and shorts, and the girls wore open cricket shirts and boys' long grey trousers, with safety-pins for clips at the bottoms.

'There's room for one behind, sonny boy,' a girl on a tandem said to me.

'It won't be a stylish marriage,' Ray said.

'That was quick,' I told Ray as we walked away from them and the boys began to sing.

'God, I like this!' said Ray. On the first rise of the dusty road through the spreading heathered common, he shaded his eyes and looked all round him, smoking like a chimney and pointing with his Irish stick at the distant clumps of trees and sights of the sea between them. 'Down there is Oxwich, but you can't see it. That's a farm. See the roof? No, there, follow my finger. This is the life,' he said.

Side by side, thrashing the low banks, we marched down the very middle of the road, and Ray saw a rabbit running. 'You wouldn't think this was near town. It's wild.'

We pointed out the birds whose names we knew, and the rest of the names we made up. I saw gulls and crows, though the crows may have been rooks, and Ray said that thrushes and swallows and skylarks flew above us as we hurried and hummed.

He stopped to pull some blades of grass. 'They should be straws,' he said, and put them in his mouth next to his pipe. 'God, the sky's blue! Think of me, in the G.W.R. when all this is about. Rabbits and fields and farms. You wouldn't think I'd suffered to look at me now. I could do anything, I could drive cows, I could plough a field.'

His father and sister and brother were dead, and his mother sat all day in a wheel-chair, crippled with arthritis. He was ten years older than I was. He had a lined and bony face and a tight, crooked mouth. His upper lip had vanished.

Alone on the long road, the common in the heat mist wasting for miles on either side, we walked on under the afternoon sun, growing thirsty and drowsy but never slowing our pace. Soon the cycling party

rode by, three boys and three girls and the one girl on the tandem, all laughing and ringing.
   'How's Shanks's pony?'
   'We'll see you on the way back.'
   'You'll be walking still.'
   'Like a crutch?' they shouted.
   Then they were gone. The dust settled again. Their bells rang faintly through the wood around the road before us. The wild common, six miles and a bit from the town, lay back without a figure on it, and, under the trees, smoking hard to keep the gnats away, we leant against a trunk and talked like men, on the edge of an untrodden place, who have not seen another man for years.
   'Do you remember Curly Parry?'
   I had seen him only two days ago in the snooker-room, but his dimpled face was fading, even as I thought of him, into the colours of our walk, the ash-white of the road, the common heathers, the green and blue of fields and fragmentary sea, and the memory of his silly voice was lost in the sounds of birds and unreasonably moving leaves in the lack of wind.
   'I wonder what he's doing now? He should get out more in the open air, he's a proper town boy. Look at us here.' Ray waved his pipe at the trees and leafy sky. 'I wouldn't change this for High Street.'
   I looked at us there: a boy and a young man, with faces, under the strange sunburn, pale from the cramped town, out of breath and hot-footed, pausing in the early afternoon on a road through a popular wood, and I could see the unaccustomed happiness in Ray's eyes and the impossible friendliness in mine, and Ray protested against his history each time he wondered or pointed in the country scene and I had more love in me than I could ever want or use.
   'Yes, look at us here,' I said, 'dawdling about. Worm's Head is twelve miles off. Don't you want to hear a tram-car, Ray? That's a wood pigeon.

See! The boys are out on the streets with the sports special now. Paper! paper! I bet you Curl's potting the red. Come on! come on!'

'Eyes right!' said Ray, 'I's b——d! Remember that story?'

Up the road and out of the wood, and a double-decker roared behind us.

'The Rhossilli bus is coming,' I said.

We both held up our sticks to stop it.

'Why did you stop the bus?' Ray said, when we were sitting upstairs. 'This was a walking holiday.'

'You stopped it as well.'

We sat in front like two more drivers.

'Can't you mind the ruts?' I said.

'You're wobbling,' said Ray.

We opened our haversacks and shared the sandwiches and hard-boiled eggs and meat paste and drank from the thermos in turns.

'When we get home don't say we took a bus,' I said. 'Pretend we walked all day. There goes Oxwich! It doesn't seem far, does it? We'd have had beards by now.'

The bus passed the cyclists crawling up a hill. 'Like a tow along?' I shouted, but they couldn't hear. The girl on the tandem was a long way behind the others.

We sat with our lunch on our laps, forgetting to steer, letting the driver in his box beneath drive where and how he liked on the switchback road, and saw grey chapels and weather-worn angels; at the feet of the hills farthest from the sea, pretty, pink cottages—horrible, I thought, to live in, for grass and trees would imprison me more securely than any jungle of packed and swarming streets and chimney-roosting roofs—and petrol pumps and hayricks and a man on a cart-horse standing stock still in a ditch, surrounded by flies.

'This is the way to see the country.'

The bus, on a narrow hill, sent two haversacked walkers bounding to the shelter of the hedge, where they stretched out their arms and drew their bellies in.

'That might have been you and me.'

We looked back happily at the men against the hedge. They climbed on to the road, slow as snails continued walking, and grew smaller.

At the entrance to Rhossilli we pushed the conductor's bell and stopped the bus, and walked, with springing steps, the few hundred yards to the village.

'We've done it in pretty good time,' said Ray.

'I think it's a record,' I said.

Laughing on the cliff above the very long golden beach, we pointed out to each other, as though the other were blind, the great rock of the Worm's Head. The sea was out. We crossed over on slipping stones and stood, at last, triumphantly on the windy top. There was monstrous, thick grass there that made us spring-heeled, and we laughed and bounced on it, scaring the sheep who ran up and down the battered sides like goats. Even on this calmest day a wind blew along the Worm. At the end of the humped and serpentine body, more gulls than I had ever seen before cried over their new dead and the droppings of ages. On the point, the sound of my quiet voice was scooped and magnified into a hollow shout, as though the wind around me had made a shell or cave, with blue, intangible roof and sides, as tall and wide as all the arched sky, and the flapping gulls were made thunderous. Standing there, legs apart, one hand on my hip, shading my eyes like Raleigh in some picture, I thought myself alone in the epileptic moment near bad sleep, when the legs grow long and sprout into the night and the heart hammers to wake the neighbours and breath is a hurricane through the elastic room. Instead of becoming small on the great rock, poised between sky and sea, I felt myself the size of a breathing building, and only Ray in the world could match my lovely bellow as I said: 'Why don't we live here always? Always and always. Build a bloody house and live like bloody kings!' The word bellowed among the squawking birds, they carried it off to the headland in the drums of their wings; like a tower, Ray pranced on the unsteady edge of a separate rock and beat about with his stick, which could turn into snakes or flames; and we sank to the ground, the rubbery, gull-limed grass, the sheep-pilled stones, the pieces of bones and feathers, and crouched at the extreme point of the Peninsula. We were still for so long that the dirty-grey gulls calmed down, and some settled near us.

Then we finished our food.

'This isn't like any other place,' I said. I was almost my own size again, five feet five and eight stone, and my voice didn't sweep any longer up to the amplifying sky. 'It could be in the middle of the sea. You could think the Worm was moving, couldn't you? Guide it to Ireland, Ray. We'll see W. B. Yeats and you can kiss the Blarney. We'll have a fight in Belfast.'

Ray looked out of place on the end of the rock. He would not make himself easy and loll in the sun and roll on to his side to stare down a precipice into the sea, but tried to sit upright as though he were in a hard chair and had nothing to do with his hands. He fiddled with his tame stick and waited for the day to be orderly, for the Head to grow paths, and for railings to shoot up on the scarred edges.

'It's too wild for a townee,' I said.

'Townee yourself! Who stopped the bus?'

'Aren't you glad we stopped it? We'd still be walking, like Felix. You're just pretending you don't like it here. You were dancing on the edge.'

'Only a couple of hops.'

'I know what it is, you don't like the furniture. There's not enough sofas and chairs,' I said.

'You think you're a country boy; you don't know a cow from a horse.'

We began to quarrel, and soon Ray felt at home again and forgot the monotonous out-of-doors. If snow had fallen suddenly he would not have noticed. He drew down into himself, and the rock, to him, became dark as a house with the blinds drawn. The sky-high shapes that had danced and bellowed at birds crept down to hide, two small town mutterers in a hollow.

I knew what was going to happen by the way Ray lowered his head and brought his shoulders up so that he looked like a man with no neck, and by the way he sucked his breath in between his teeth. He stared at his dusty white shoes and I knew what shapes his imagination made of them: they were the feet of a man dead in bed, and he was going to talk about his brother. Sometimes, leaning against a fence when we watched football, I caught him staring at his own thin hand: he was thinning it more and more, removing the flesh, seeing Harry's hand in front of him, with the bones appearing through the sensitive skin. If he lost the world around him for a moment, if I left him alone, if he cast his eyes down, if his hand lost its grip on the hard, real fence or the hot bowl of his pipe, he would be back in ghastly bedrooms, carrying cloths and basins and listening for handbells.

'I've never seen such a lot of gulls,' I said. 'Have you ever seen such a lot? Such a lot of gulls. You try and count them. Two of them are fighting up there; look, pecking each other like hens in the air. What'll you bet the big one wins? Old dirty beak! I wouldn't like to have had his dinner, a bit of sheep and dead gull.' I swore at myself for saying the word 'dead.' 'Wasn't it gay in town this morning?' I said.

Ray stared at his hand. Nothing could stop him now. 'Wasn't it gay in town this morning? Everybody laughing and smiling in their summer outfits. The kids were playing and everybody was happy; they almost had the band out. I used to hold my father down on the bed when he had fits. I had to change the sheets twice a day for my brother, there was blood on everything. I watched him getting thinner and thinner; in the end you could lift him up with one hand. And his wife wouldn't go to see him because he coughed in her face. Mother couldn't move, and I had to cook as well, cook and nurse and change the sheets and hold father down when he got mad. It's embittered my outlook,' he said.

'But you loved the walk, you enjoyed yourself on the common. It's a wonderful day, Ray. I'm sorry about your brother. Let's explore. Let's climb down to the sea. Perhaps there's a cave with prehistoric drawings, and we can write an article and make a fortune. Let's climb down.'

'My brother used to ring a bell for me; he could only whisper. He used to say: "Ray, look at my legs. Are they thinner to-day?"'

'The sun's going down. Let's climb.'

'Father thought I was trying to murder him when I held him on the bed. I was holding him down when he died, and he rattled. Mother was in the kitchen in her chair, but she knew he was dead and she started screaming for my sister. Brenda was in a sanatorium in Craigynos. Harry rang the bell in his bedroom when mother started, but I couldn't go to him, and father was dead in the bed.'

'I'm going to climb to the sea,' I said. 'Are you coming?'

He got up out of the hollow into the open world again and followed me slowly over the point and down the steep side; the gulls rose in a storm. I clung to dry, spiked bushes but the roots came out; a foothold crumbled, a crevice for the fingers broke as I groped in it; I scrambled on to a black, flat-backed rock whose head, like a little Worm's, curved out of the sea a few perilous steps away from me, and, drenched by flying water, I gazed up to see Ray and a shower of stones falling. He landed at my side.

'I thought I was done for,' he said, when he had stopped shaking. 'I could see all my past life in a flash.'

'All of it?'

'Well, nearly. I saw my brother's face clear as yours.'

We watched the sun set.

'Like an orange.'

'Like a tomato.'

'Like a goldfish bowl.'

We went one better than the other, describing the sun. The sea beat on our rock, soaked our trouser-legs, stung our cheeks. I took off my shoes and held Ray's hand and slid down the rock on my belly to trail my feet in the sea. Then Ray slid down, and I held him fast while he kicked up water.

'Come back now,' I said, pulling his hand.

'No, no,' he said, 'this is delicious. Let me keep my feet in a bit more. It's warm as the baths.' He kicked and grunted and slapped the rock in a frenzy with his other hand, pretending to drown. 'Don't save me!' he cried. 'I'm drowning! I'm drowning!'

I pulled him back, and in his struggles he brushed a shoe off the rock. We fished it out. It was full of water.

'Never mind, it was worth it. I haven't paddled since I was six. I can't tell you how much I enjoyed it.'

He had forgotten about his father and his brother, but I knew that once his joy in the wild, warm water was over he would return to the painful house and see his brother growing thinner. I had heard Harry die so many times, and the mad father was as familiar to me as Ray himself. I knew every cough and cry, every clawing at the air.

'I'm going to paddle once a day from now on,' Ray said. 'I'm going to go down to the sands every evening and have a good paddle. I'm going to splash about and get wet up to my knees. I don't care who laughs.'

He sat still for a minute, thinking gravely of this. 'When I wake up in the mornings there's nothing to look forward to, except on Saturdays,' he said then, 'or when I come up to your house for Lexicon. I may as well be dead. But now I'll be able to wake up and think: "This evening I'm going to splash about in the sea." I'm going to do it again now.' He rolled up his wet trousers and slid down the rock. 'Don't let go.'

As he kicked his legs in the sea, I said: 'This is a rock at the world's end. We're all alone. It all belongs to us, Ray. We can have anybody we like here and keep everybody else away. Who do you wish was with us?'

He was too busy to answer, splashing and snorting, blowing as though his head were under, making circular commotions in the water or lazily skimming the surface with his toes.

'Who would you like to be here on the rock with us?'

He was stretched out like a dead man, his feet motionless in the sea, his mouth on the rim of a rock pool, his hand clutched round my foot.

'I wish George Gray was with us,' I said. 'He's the man from London who's come to live in Norfolk Street. You don't know him. He's the most curious man I ever met, queerer than Oscar Thomas, and I thought nobody could ever be queerer than that. George Gray wears glasses, but there's no glass in them, only the frames. You wouldn't know until you came near him. He does all sorts of things. He's a cat's doctor and he goes to somewhere in Sketty every morning to help a woman put her clothes on. She's an old widow, he said, and she can't dress by herself. I don't know how he came to know her. He's only been in town for a month. He's a B.A., too. The things he's got in his pockets! Pincers, and scissors for cats, and lots of diaries. He read me some of the diaries, about the jobs he did in London. He used to go to bed with a policewoman and she used to pay him. She used to go to bed in her uniform. I've never met such a queer man. I wish he was here now. Who do you wish was with us, Ray?'

Ray began to move his feet again, kicking them out straight behind him and bringing them down hard on the water, and then stirring the water about.

'I wish Gwilym was here, too,' I said. 'I've told you about him. He could give a sermon to the sea. This is the very place, there isn't anywhere as lonely as this.' Oh, the beloved sunset! Oh, the terrible sea! Pity the sailors, pity the sinners, pity Raymond Price and me! Oh, the evening is coming like a cloud! Amen. Amen. 'Who do you wish, Ray?'

'I wish my brother was with us,' Ray said. He climbed on to the flat of the rock and dried his feet. 'I wish Harry was here. I wish he was here now, at this moment, on this rock.'

The sun was nearly right down, halved by the shadowed sea. Cold came up, spraying out of the sea, and I could make a body for it, icy antlers, a dripping tail, a rippling face with fishes passing across it. A wind, cornering the Head, chilled through our summer shirts, and the sea began to cover our rock quickly, our rock already covered with friends, with living and dead, racing against the darkness. We did not speak as we climbed. I thought: 'If we open our mouths we'll both say: "Too late, it's too late."' We ran over the springboard grass and the scraping rock needles, down the hollow in which Ray had talked about blood, up rustling humps, and along the ragged flat. We stood on the beginning of the Head and looked down, though both of us could have said, without looking: 'The sea is in.'

The sea was in. The slipping stepping-stones were gone. On the mainland, in the dusk, some little figures beckoned to us. Seven clear figures, jumping and calling. I thought they were the cyclists.

Old Garbo

Mr Farr trod delicately and disgustedly down the dark, narrow stairs like a man on mice. He knew, without looking or slipping, that vicious boys had littered the darkest corners with banana peel; and when he reached the lavatory, the basins would be choked and the chains snapped on purpose. He remembered 'Mr Farr, no father' scrawled in brown, and the day the sink was full of blood that nobody admitted having lost. A girl rushed past him up the stairs, knocked the papers out of his hand, did not apologize, and the loose meg of his cigarette burned his lower lip as he failed to open the lavatory door. I heard from inside his protest and rattlings, the sing-song whine of his voice, the stamping of his small, patent-leather shoes, his favourite swear-words—he swore, violently and privately, like a collier used to thinking in the dark—and I let him in.

'Do you always lock the door?' he asked, scurrying to the tiled wall.

'It stuck,' I said.

He shivered, and buttoned.

He was the senior reporter, a great shorthand writer, a chain-smoker, a bitter drinker, very humorous, round-faced and round-bellied, with dart holes in his nose. Once, I thought as I stared at him then in the lavatory of the offices of the *Tawe News*, he might have been a mincing-mannered man, with a strut and a cane to balance it, a watch-chain across the waistcoat, a gold tooth, even, perhaps a flower from his own garden in his buttonhole. But now each attempt at a precise gesture was caked and soaked before it began; when he placed the tips of his thumb and forefinger together, you saw only the cracked nails in mourning and the Woodbine stains. He gave me a cigarette and shook his coat to hear matches.

'Here's a light, Mr Farr,' I said.

It was good to keep in with him; he covered all the big stories, the occasional murder, such as when Thomas O'Connor used a bottle on his wife—but that was before my time—the strikes, the best fires. I wore my cigarette as he did, a hanging badge of bad habits.

'Look at that word on the wall,' he said. 'Now that's ugly. There's a time and a place.'

Winking at me, scratching his bald patch as though the thought came from there, he said: 'Mr Solomon wrote that.'

Mr Solomon was the news editor and a Wesleyan.

'Old Solomon,' said Mr Farr, 'he'd cut every baby in half just for pleasure.'

I smiled and said: 'I bet he would!' But I wished that I could have answered in such a way as to show for Mr Solomon the disrespect I did not feel. This was a great male moment, and the most enjoyable since I had begun work three weeks before: leaning against the cracked tiled wall, smoking and smiling, looking down at my shoe scraping circles on the wet floor, sharing a small wickedness with an old, important man. I should have been writing up last night's performance of *The Crucifixion* or loitering, with my new hat on one side, through the Christmas-Saturday-crowded town in the hopes of an accident.

'You must come along with me one night,' Mr Farr said slowly. 'We'll go down the "Fishguard" on the docks; you can see the sailors knitting there in the public bar. Why not to-night? And there's shilling women in the "Lord Jersey." You stick to Woodbines, like me.'

He washed his hands as a young boy does, wiping the dirt on the roll-towel, stared in the mirror over the basin, twirled the ends of his moustache, and saw them droop again immediately after.

'Get to work,' he said.

I walked into the lobby, leaving him with his face pressed to the glass and one finger exploring his bushy nostrils.

It was nearly eleven o'clock, and time for a cocoa or a Russian tea in the Café Royal, above a tobacconist's in High Street, where junior clerks and shop assistants and young men working in their fathers' offices or articled to stockbrokers and solicitors met every morning for gossip and stories. I made my way through the crowds: the Valley men, up for the football; the country shoppers; the window gazers; the silent, shabby men at the corners of the packed streets, standing in isolation in the rain; the press of mothers and prams; old women in black, brooched dresses carrying frails; smart girls with shining mackintoshes and splashed stockings; little, dandy lascars, bewildered by the weather; business men with wet spats; through a mushroom forest of umbrellas; and all the time I thought of the paragraphs I would never write. I'll put you all in a story by and by.

Mrs Constable, laden and red with shopping, recognized me as she charged out of Woolworth's like a bull. 'I haven't seen your mother for ages! Oh! this Christmas rush! Remember me to Florrie. I'm going to have a cup of tea at the "Modern." There,' she said, 'I've lost a pan!'

I saw Percy Lewis, who put chewing gum in my hair at school.

A tall man stared at the doorway of a hat shop, resisting the crowds, standing hard and still. All the moving irrelevancies of good news grew and acted around me as I reached the café entrance and climbed the stairs.

'What's for you, Mr Swaffer?'

'The usual, please.' Cocoa and free biscuit.

Most of the boys were there already. Some wore the outlines of moustaches, others had sideboards and crimped hair, some smoked curved pipes and talked with them gripped between their teeth, there were pin-stripe trousers and hard collars, one daring bowler.

'Sit by here,' said Leslie Bird. He was in the boots at Dan Lewis's.

'Been to the flicks this week, Thomas?'

'Yes. The Regal. *White Lies*. Damned good show, too! Connie Bennett was great! Remember her in the foam-bath, Leslie?'

'Too much foam for me, old man.'

The broad vowels of the town were narrowed in, the rise and fall of the family accent was caught and pressed.

At the top window of the International Stores across the street a group of uniformed girls were standing with tea-cups in their hands. One of them waved a handkerchief. I wondered if she waved it to me. 'There's that dark piece again,' I said. 'She's got her eye on you.'

'They look all right in their working clothes,' he said. 'You catch them when they're all dolled up, they're awful. I knew a little nurse once, she looked a peach in her uniform, really refined; no, really, I mean. I picked her up on the prom one night. She was in her Sunday best. There's a difference; she looked like a bit of Marks and Spencer's.' As he talked he was looking through the window with the corners of his eyes.

The girl waved again, and turned away to giggle.

'Pretty cheap!' he said.

I said: 'And little Audrey laughed and laughed.'

He took out a plated cigarette case. 'Present,' he said. 'I bet my uncle with three balls has it in a week. Have a best Turkish.'

His matches were marked Allsopps. 'Got them from the "Carlton,"' he said. 'Pretty girl behind the bar; knows her onions. You've never been there, have you? Why don't you drop in for one to-night? Gil Morris'll be there, too. We usually sink a couple Saturdays. There's a hop at the "Melba."'

'Sorry,' I said. 'I'm going out with our senior reporter. Some other time, Leslie. So long!'

I paid my threepence.

'Good morning, Cassie.'

'Good morning, Hannen.'

The rain had stopped and High Street shone. Walking on the tramlines, a neat man held his banner high and prominently feared the Lord. I knew him as a Mr Matthews, who had been saved some years ago from British port and who now walked every night, in rubber shoes with a prayer book and a flashlight, through the lanes. There went Mr Evans the Produce through the side-door of the 'Bugle.' Three typists rushed by for lunch, poached egg and milkshake, leaving a lavender scent. Should I take the long way through the Arcade, and stop to look at the old man with the broken, empty pram, who always stood there, by the music store, and who would take off his cap and set his hair alight for a penny? It was only a trick to amuse boys, and I took the short cut down Chapel Street, on the edge of the slum called the Strand, past the enticing Italian chip shop where young men who had noticing parents bought twopenny-worth on late nights to hide their breath before the last tram home. Then up the narrow office stairs and into the reporters' room.

Mr Solomon was shouting down the telephone. I heard the last words: 'You're just a dreamer, Williams.' He put the receiver down. 'That boy's a buddy dreamer,' he said to no one. He never swore.

I finished my report of *The Crucifixion* and handed it to Mr Farr.

'Too much platitudinous verbosity.'

Half an hour later, Ted Williams, dressed to golf, sidled in, smiling, thumbed his nose at Mr Solomon's back, and sat quietly in a corner with a nail-file.

I whispered: 'What was he slanging you for?'

'I went out on a suicide, a tram conductor called Hopkins, and the widow made me stay and have a cup of tea. That's all.' He was very winning in his ways, more like a girl than a man who dreamed of Fleet Street and spent his summer fortnight walking up and down past the *Daily Express* office and looking for celebrities in the pubs.

Saturday was my free afternoon. It was one o'clock and time to leave, but I stayed on; Mr Farr said nothing. I pretended to be busy, scribbling words and caricaturing with no likeness Mr Solomon's toucan profile and the snub copy-boy who whistled out of tune behind the windows of the telephone box. I wrote my name, 'Reporters' Room, *Tawe News*, Tawe, South Wales, England, Europe, The Earth.' And a list of books I had not written: 'Land of My Fathers, a Study of the Welsh Character in all its aspects'; 'Eighteen, a Provincial Autobiography'; 'The Merciless Ladies, a Novel.' Still Mr Farr did not look up. I wrote 'Hamlet'. Surely Mr Farr, stubbornly transcribing his council notes had not forgotten. I heard Mr Solomon mutter, leaning over his shoulder: 'To aitch with Alderman Daniels.' Half past one. Ted was in a dream. I spent a long time putting on my overcoat, tied my Old Grammarian's scarf one way and then another.

'Some people are too lazy to take their half-days off,' said Mr Farr suddenly. 'Six o'clock in the "Lamps"' back bar.' He did not turn round nor stop writing.

'Going for a nice walk?' asked my mother.

'Yes, on the common. Don't keep tea waiting.'

I went to the Plaza. 'Press,' I said to the girl with the Tyrolean hat and skirt.

'There's been two reporters this week.'

'Special notice.'

She showed me to a seat. During the educational film, with the rude seeds hugging and sprouting in front of my eyes and plants like arms and legs, I thought of the bob women and the pansy sailors in the dives. There might be a quarrel with razors, and once Ted Williams found a lip outside the Mission to Seamen. It had a small moustache. The sinuous plants danced on the screen. If only Tawe were a larger seatown, there would be curtained rooms underground with blue films. The potato's life came to an end. Then I entered an American college and danced with the president's daughter. The hero, called Lincoln, tall and dark with good teeth, I displaced quickly, and the girl spoke my name as she held his shadow, the singing college chorus in sailors' hats and bathing dresses called me big boy and king, Jack Oakie and I sped up the field, and on the shoulders of the crowd the president's daughter and I brought across the shifting-coloured curtain with a kiss that left me giddy and bright-eyed as I walked out of the cinema into the strong lamplight and the new rain.

A whole wet hour to waste in the crowds. I watched the queue outside the Empire and studied the posters of *Nuit de Paris*, and thought of the long legs and startling faces of the chorus girls I had seen walking arm in arm, earlier that week, up and down the streets in the winter sunshine, their mouths, I remembered remarking and treasuring for the first page of 'The Merciless Ladies' that was never begun, like crimson scars, their hair raven-black or silver; their scent and paint reminded me of the hot and chocolate-coloured East, their eyes were pools. Lola de Kenway, Babs Courcey, Ramona Day would be with me all my life. Until I died, of a wasting, painless disease, and spoke my prepared last words, they would always walk with me, recalling me to my dead youth in the vanished High Street nights when the shop windows were blazing, and singing came out of the pubs, and sirens from the Hafod sat in the steaming chip shops with their handbags on their knees and their ear-rings rattling. I stopped to look at the window of Dirty Black's, the Fancy Man, but it was innocent; there were only itching and sneezing powders, stink bombs, rubber pens, and Charlie masks; all the novelties were inside, but I dared not go in for fear a woman should serve me, Mrs Dirty Black with a moustache and knowing eyes, or a thin, dog-faced girl I saw there once, who winked and smelt of seaweed. In the market I bought pink cachous. You never knew.

The back room of 'The Three Lamps' was full of elderly men. Mr Farr had not arrived. I leant against the bar, between an alderman and a solicitor, drinking bitter, wishing that my father could see me now and glad, at the same time, that he was visiting Uncle A. in Aberavon. He could not fail to see that I was a boy no longer, nor fail to be angry at the angle of my fag and my hat and the threat of the clutched tankard. I liked the taste of beer, its live, white lather, its brass-bright depths, the sudden world through the wet-brown walls of the glass, the tilted rush to the lips and the slow swallowing down to the lapping belly, the salt on the tongue, the foam at the corners.

'Same again, miss.' She was middle-aged. 'One for you, miss?'

'Not during hours, ta all the same.'

'You're welcome.'

Was that an invitation to drink with her afterwards, to wait at the back door until she glided out, and then to walk through the night, along the promenade and sands, on to a soft dune where couples lay loving under their coats and looking at the Mumbles lighthouse? She was plump and plain, her netted hair was auburn and wisped with grey. She gave me my change like a mother giving her boy pennies for the pictures, and I would not go out with her if she put cream on it.

Mr Farr hurried down High Street, savagely refusing laces and matches, averting his eyes from the shabby crowds. He knew that the poor and the sick and the ugly, unwanted people were so close around him that, with one look of recognition, one gesture of sympathy, he would be lost among them and the evening would be spoiled for ever.

'You're a pint man then,' he said at my elbow.

'Good evening, Mr Farr. Only now and then for a change. What's yours? Dirty night,' I said.

Safe in a prosperous house, out of the way of the rain and the unsettling streets, where the poor and the past could not touch him, he took his glass lazily in the company of business and professional men and raised it to the light. 'It's going to get dirtier,' he said. 'You wait till the "Fishguard." Here's health! You can see the sailors knitting there. And the old fish-girls in the "Jersey." Got to go to the w. for a breath of fresh air.'

Mr Evans the Produce came in quickly through a side door hidden by curtains, whispered his drink, shielded it with his overcoat, swallowed it in secrecy.

'Similar,' said Mr Farr, 'and half for his nibs.'

The bar was too high class to look like Christmas. A notice said 'No Ladies.'

We left Mr Evans gulping in his tent.

Children screamed in Goat Street, and one boy, out of season, pulled my sleeve, crying: 'Penny for the guy!' Big women in men's caps barricaded their doorways, and a posh girl gave us the wink at the corner of the green iron convenience opposite the Carlton Hotel. We entered to music, the bar was hung with ribbons and balloons, a tubercular tenor clung to the piano, behind the counter Leslie Bird's pretty barmaid was twitting a group of young men who leant far over and asked to see her garters and invited her to gins and limes and lonely midnight walks and moist adventures in the cinema. Mr Farr sneered down his glass as I watched the young men enviously and saw how much she liked their ways, how she slapped their hands lightly and wriggled back, in pride of her prettiness and gaiety, to pull the beer-handles.

'Toop little Twms from the Valleys. There'll be some puking tonight,' he said with pleasure.

Other young men, sleek-haired, pale, and stocky, with high cheekbones and deep eyes, bright ties, double-breasted waistcoats and wide trousers, some pocked from the pits, their broad hands scarred and damaged, all exultantly half-drunk, stood singing round the piano, and the tenor with the fallen chest led in a clear voice. Oh! to be able to join in the suggestive play or the rocking choir, to shout *Bread of Heaven*, with my shoulders back and my arms linked with Little Moscow, or to be called 'saucy' and 'a one' as I joked and ogled at the counter, making innocent, dirty love that could come to nothing among the spilt beer and piling glasses.

'Let's get away from the bloody nightingales,' said Mr Farr.

'Too much bloody row,' I said.

'Now we're coming to somewhere.' We crawled down Strand alleys by the side of the mortuary, through a gas-lit lane where hidden babies cried together, and reached the 'Fishguard' door as a man, muffled like Mr Evans, slid out in front of us with a bottle or a black-jack in one gloved hand. The bar was empty. An old man whose hands trembled sat behind the counter, staring at his turnip watch.

'Merry Christmas, Pa.'
'Good evening, Mr F.'
'Drop of rum, Pa.'
A red bottle shook over two glasses.
'Very special poison, son.'
'This'll make your eyes bulge,' said Mr Farr.

My iron head stood high and firm, no sailors' rum could rot the rock of my belly. Poor Leslie Bird the port-sipper, and little Gil Morris who marked dissipation under his eyes with a blacklead every Saturday night, I wished they could have seen me now, in the dark, stunted room with photographs of boxers peeling on the wall.

'More poison, Pa,' I said.

'Where's the company to-night? gone to the Riviera?'

'They're in the snuggery, Mr F., there's a party for Mrs Prothero's daughter.'

In the back room, under a damp royal family, a row of black-dressed women on a hard bench sat laughing and crying, short glasses lined by their Guinnesses. On an opposite bench two men in jerseys drank appreciatively, nodding at the emotions of the women. And on the one chair, in the middle of the room, an old woman, with a bonnet tied under her chins, a feather boa, and white gym-shoes, tittered and wept above the rest. We sat on the men's bench. One of the two touched his cap with a sore hand.

'What's the party, Jack?' asked Mr Farr. 'Meet my colleague, Mr Thomas; this is Jack Stiff, the mortuary keeper.'

Jack Stiff spoke from the side of his mouth. 'It's Mrs Prothero there. We call her Old Garbo because she isn't like her, see. She had a message from the hospital about an hour ago, Mrs Harris's Winifred brought it here, to say her second daughter's died in pod.'

'Baby girl dead, too,' said the man at his side.

'So all the old girls came round to sympathize, and they made a big collection for her, and now she's beginning to drink it up and treating round. We've had a couple of pints from her already.'

'Shameful!'

The rum burned and kicked in the hot room, but my head felt tough as a hill and I could write twelve books before morning and roll the 'Carlton' barmaid, like a barrel, the length of Tawe sands.

'Drinks for the troops!'

Before a new audience, the women cried louder, patting Mrs Prothero's knees and hands, adjusting her bonnet, praising her dead daughter.

'What'll you have, Mrs Prothero, dear?'

'No, have it with me, dear, best in the house.'

'Well, a Guinness tickles my fancy.'

'And a little something in it, dear.'

'Just for Margie's sake, then.'

'Think if she was here now, dear, singing *One of the Ruins* or *Cockles and Mussels*; she had a proper madam's voice.'

'Oh, don't, Mrs Harris!'

'There, we're only bucking you up. Grief killed the cat, Mrs Prothero. Let's have a song together, dear.'

'The pale moon was rising above the grey mountain,
The sun was declining beneath the blue sea,
When I strolled with my love to the pure crystal fountain,'
Mrs Prothero sang.

'It was her daughter's favourite song,' said Jack Stiff's friend.

Mr Farr tapped me on the shoulder; his hand fell slowly from a great height and his thin, bird's voice spoke from a whirring circle on the ceiling. 'A drop of out-of-doors for you and me.' The gamps and bonnets, the white gym-shoes, the bottles and the mildew king, the singing mortuary man, the *Rose of Tralee*, swam together in the snuggery; two small men, Mr Farr and his twin brother, led me on an ice-rink to the door, and the night air slapped me down. The evening happened suddenly. A wall slumped over and knocked off my trilby; Mr Farr's brother disappeared under the cobbles. Here came a wall like a buffalo; dodge him, son. Have a drop of angostura, have a drop of brandy, Fernet Branca, Polly, Ooo! the mother's darling! have a hair of the dog.

'Feeling better now?'

I sat in a plush chair I had never seen before, sipping a mothball drink and appreciating an argument between Ted Williams and Mr Farr. Mr Farr was saying sternly: 'You came in here to look for sailors.'

'No, I didn't then,' said Ted. 'I came for local colour.'

The notices on the walls were: '"The Lord Jersey." Prop.: Titch Thomas.' 'No Betting.' 'No Swearing, B—— you.' 'The Lord helps Himself, but you mustn't.' 'No Ladies allowed, except Ladies.'

'This is a funny pub,' I said. 'See the notices?'

'Okay now?'

'I'm feeling upsydaisy.'

'There's a pretty girl for you. Look, she's giving you the glad.'

'But she's got no nose.'

My drink, like winking, had turned itself into beer. A hammer tapped. 'Order! order!' At a sound in a new saloon a collarless chairman with a cigar called on Mr Jenkins to provide *The Lily of Laguna*.

'By request,' said Mr Jenkins.

'Order! order! for Katie Sebastopol Street. What is it, Katie?'

She sang the National Anthem.

'Mr Fred Jones will supply his usual dirty one.'

A broken baritone voice spoiled the chorus; I recognized it as my own, and drowned it.

A girl of the Salvation Army avoided the arms of two firemen and sold them a *War Cry*.

A young man with a dazzling handkerchief round his head, black and white holiday shoes with holes for the toes, and no socks, danced until the bar cried: 'Mabel!'

Ted clapped at my side. 'That's style! "Nijinsky of the Night-world," there's a story! Wonder if I can get an interview?'

'Half a crack,' said Mr Farr.

'Don't make me cross.'

A wind from the docks tore up the street, I heard the rowdy dredger in the bay and a boat blowing to come in, the gas-lamps bowed and bent, then again smoke closed about the stained walls with George and Mary dripping above the women's bench, and Jack Stiff whispered, holding his hand in front of him like the paw of an animal: 'Old Garbo's gone.'

The sad and jolly women huddled together.

'Mrs Harris's little girl got the message wrong. Old Garbo's daughter's right as rain, the baby was born dead. Now the old girls want their money back, but they can't find Garbo anywhere.' He licked his hand. 'I know where she's gone.'

His friend said: 'To a boozer over the bridge.'

In low voices the women reviled Mrs Prothero, liar, adulteress, mother of bastards, thief.

'She got you know what.'

'Never cured it.'

'Got Charlie tattooed on her.'

'Three and eight she owes me.'

'Two and ten.'

'Money for my teeth.'

'One and a tanner out of my Old Age.'

Who kept filling my glass? Beer ran down my cheek and my collar. My mouth was full of saliva. The bench spun. The cabin of the 'Fishguard' tilted. Mr Farr retreated slowly; the telescope twisted, and his face, with wide and hairy nostrils, breathed against mine.

'Mr Thomas is going to get sick.'
'Mind your brolly, Mrs Arthur.'
'Take his head.'

The last tram clanked home. I did not have the penny for the fare. 'You get off here. Careful!' The revolving hill to my father's house reached to the sky. Nobody was up. I crept to a wild bed, and the wallpaper lakes converged and sucked me down.

Sunday was a quiet day, though St Mary's bells, a mile away, rang on, long after church time, in the holes of my head. Knowing that I would never drink again, I lay in bed until midday dinner and remembered the unsteady shapes and far-off voices of the ten o'clock town. I read the newspapers. All news was bad that morning, but an article called 'Our Lord was a Flower-lover' moved me to tears of bewilderment and contrition. I excused myself from the Sunday joint and three vegetables.

In the park in the afternoon I sat alone near the deserted bandstand. I caught a ball of waste paper that the wind blew down the gravel path towards the rockery, and, straightening it out and holding it on my knee, wrote the first three lines of a poem without hope. A dog nosed me out where I crouched, behind a bare tree in the cold, and rubbed its nose against my hand. 'My only friend,' I said. It stayed with me up to the early dusk, sniffing and scratching.

On Monday morning, with shame and hate, afraid to look at them again, I destroyed the article and the poem, throwing the pieces on to the top of the wardrobe, and I told Leslie Bird in the tram to the office: 'You should have been with us, Saturday. Christ!'

Early on Tuesday night, which was Christmas Eve, I walked, with a borrowed half-crown, into the back room of the 'Fishguard.' Jack Stiff was alone. The women's bench was covered with sheets of newspaper. A bunch of balloons hung from the lamp.

'Here's health!'
'Merry Christmas!'

'Where's Mrs Prothero?'

His hand was bandaged now. 'Oh! You haven't heard? She spent all the collection money. She took it over the bridge to the "Heart's Delight." She didn't let one of the old girls see her. It was over a pound. She'd spent a lot of it before they found her daughter wasn't dead. She couldn't face them then. Have this one with me. So she finished it up by stop-tap Monday. Then a couple of men from the banana boats saw her walking across the bridge, and she stopped half-way. But they weren't in time.'

'Merry Christmas!'

'We got a pair of gym-shoes on our slab.'

None of Old Garbo's friends came in that night.

When I showed this story a long time later to Mr Farr, he said: 'You got it all wrong. You got the people mixed. The boy with the handkerchief danced in the "Jersey." Fred Jones was singing in the "Fishguard." Never mind. Come and have one to-night in the "Nelson." There's a girl down there who'll show you where the sailor bit her. And there's a policeman who knew Jack Johnson.'

'I'll put them all in a story by and by,' I said.

One Warm Saturday

The young man in a sailor's jersey, sitting near the summer huts to see the brown and white women coming out and the groups of pretty-faced girls with pale vees and scorched backs who picked their way delicately on ugly, red-toed feet over the sharp stones to the sea, drew on the sand a large, indented woman's figure; and a naked child, just out of the sea, ran over it and shook water, marking on the figure two wide wet eyes and a hole in the footprinted middle. He rubbed the woman away and drew a paunched man; the child ran over it, tossing her hair, and shook a row of buttons down its belly and a line of drops, like piddle in a child's drawing, between the long legs stuck with shells.

    In a huddle of picnicking women and their children, stretched out limp and damp in the sweltering sun or fussing over paper carriers or building castles that were at once destroyed by the tattered march of other picnickers to different pieces of the beach, among the ice-cream cries, the angrily happy shouts of boys playing ball, and the screams of girls as the sea rose to their waists, the young man sat alone with the shadows of his failure at his side. Some silent husbands, with rolled up trousers and suspenders dangling, paddled slowly on the border of the sea, paddling women, in thick, black picnic dresses, laughed at their own legs, dogs chased stones, and one proud boy rode the water on a rubber seal. The young man, in his wilderness, saw the holiday Saturday set down before him, false and pretty, as a flat picture under the vulgar sun; the disporting families with paper bags, buckets and spades, parasols and bottles, the happy, hot, and aching girls with sunburn liniments in their bags, the bronzed young men with chests, and the envious, white young men in waistcoats, the thin, pale, hairy, pathetic legs of the husbands silently walking through the water, the plump and curly, shaven-headed and bowed-backed children up to no sense with unrepeatable delight in the dirty sand, moved him, he thought dramatically in his isolation, to an old shame and pity; outside all holiday, like a young man doomed for ever to the company of his maggots, beyond the high and ordinary, sweating, sun-awakened power and stupidity of the summer flesh on a day and a world out, he caught the ball that a small boy had whacked into the air with a tin tray, and rose to throw it back.

The boy invited him to play. A friendly family stood waiting some way off, the tousled women with their dresses tucked in their knickers, the bare-footed men in shirtsleeves, a number of children in slips and cut-down underwear. He bowled bitterly to a father standing with a tray before a wicket of hats. 'The lone wolf playing ball,' he said to himself as the tray whirled. Chasing the ball towards the sea, passing undressing women with a rush and a wink, tripping over a castle into a coil of wet girls lying like snakes, soaking his shoes as he grabbed the ball off a wave, he felt his happiness return in a boast of the body, and, 'Look out, Duckworth, here's a fast one coming,' he cried to the mother behind the hats. The ball bounced on a boy's head. In and out of the scattered families, among the sandwiches and clothes, uncles and mothers fielded the bouncing ball. A bald man, with his shirt hanging out, returned it in the wrong direction, and a collie carried it into the sea. Now it was mother's turn with the tray. Tray and ball together flew over her head. An uncle in a panama smacked the ball to the dog, who swam with it out of reach. They offered the young man egg-and-cress sandwiches and warm stout, and he and an uncle and a father sat down on the *Evening Post* until the sea touched their feet.

Alone again, hot and unhappy, for the boasting minute when he ran among the unknown people lying and running loudly at peace was struck away, like a ball, he said, into the sea, he walked to a space on the beach where a hell-fire preacher on a box marked 'Mr Matthews' was talking to a congregation of expressionless women. Boys with peashooters sat quietly near him. A ragged man collected nothing in a cap. Mr Matthews shook his cold hands, stormed at the holiday, and cursed the summer from his shivering box. He cried for a new warmth. The strong sun shone into his bones, and he buttoned his coat collar. Valley children, with sunken, impudent eyes, quick tongues and singing voices, chests thin as shells, gathered round the Punch and Judy and the Stop Me tricycles, and he denied them all. He contradicted the girls in their underclothes combing and powdering, and the modest girls cleverly dressing under tents of towels.

As Mr Matthews cast down the scarlet town, drove out the bare-bellied boys who danced around the ice-cream man, and wound the girls' sunburnt thighs about with his black overcoat—'Down! down!' he cried, 'the night is upon us'—the young man in dejection stood, with a shadow at his shoulder, and thought of Porthcawl's Coney Beach, where his friends were rocking with girls on the Giant Racer or tearing in the Ghost Train down the skeletons' tunnel. Leslie Bird would have his arms full of coco-nuts. Brenda was with Herbert at the rifle-range. Gil Morris was buying Molly a cocktail with a cherry at the 'Esplanade.' Here he stood, listening to Mr Matthews, the retired drinker, crying darkness on the evening sands, with money hot in his pocket and Saturday burning away.

In his loneliness he had refused their invitations. Herbert, in his low, red sports car, G. B. at the back, a sea-blown nymph on the radiator, called at his father's house, but he said: 'I'm not in the mood, old man. I'm going to spend a quiet day. Enjoy yourselves. Don't take too much pop.' Only waiting for the sun to set, he stood in the sad circle with the pleasureless women who were staring at a point in the sky behind their prophet, and wished the morning back. Oh, boy! to be wasting his money now on the rings and ranges of the fair, to be sitting in the chromium lounge with a short worth one and six and a Turkish cigarette, telling the latest one to the girls, seeing the sun, through the palms in the lounge window, sink over the promenade, over the Bath chairs, the cripples and widows, the beach-trousered, kerchiefed, week-end wives, the smart, kiss-curled girls with plain and spectacled girl friends, the innocent, swaggering, loud bad boys, and the poms at the ankles, and the cycling sweet-men. Ronald had sailed to Ilfracombe on the *Lady Moira*, and, in the thick saloon, with a party from Brynhyfryd, he'd be knocking back nips without a thought that on the sands at home his friend was alone and pussyfoot at six o'clock, and the evening dull as a chapel. All his friends had vanished into their pleasures.

He thought: Poets live and walk with their poems; a man with visions needs no other company; Saturday is a crude day; I must go home and sit in my bedroom by the boiler. But he was not a poet living and walking, he was a young man in a sea town on a warm bank holiday, with two pounds to spend; he had no visions, only two pounds and a small body with its feet on the littered sand; serenity was for old men; and he moved away, over the railway points, on to the tram-lined road.

He snarled at the flower clock in Victoria Gardens.

'And what shall a prig do now?' he said aloud, causing a young woman on a bench opposite the white-tiled urinal to smile and put her novel down.

She had chestnut hair arranged high on her head in an old-fashioned way, in loose coils and a bun, and a Woolworth's white rose grew out of it and drooped to touch her ear. She wore a white frock with a red paper flower pinned on the breast, and rings and bracelets that came from a fun-fair stall. Her eyes were small and quite green.

He marked, carefully and coldly in one glance, all the unusual details of her appearance; it was the calm, unstartled certainty of her bearing before his glance from head to foot, the innocent knowledge, in her smile and the set of her head, that she was defended by her gentleness and accessible strangeness against all rude encounters and picking looks, that made his fingers tremble. Though her frock was long and the collar high, she could as well be naked there on the blistered bench. Her smile confessed her body bare and spotless and willing and warm under the cotton, and she waited without guilt.

How beautiful she is, he thought, with his mind on words and his eyes on her hair and red and white skin, how beautifully she waits for me, though she does not know she is waiting and I can never tell her.

He had stopped and was staring. Like a confident girl before a camera, she sat smiling, her hands folded, her head slightly to one side so that the rose brushed her neck. She accepted his admiration. The girl in a million took his long look to herself, and cherished his stupid love.

Midges flew into his mouth. He hurried on shamefully. At the gates of the Gardens he turned to see her for the last time on earth. She had lost her calm with his abrupt and awkward going, and stared in confusion after him. One hand was raised as though to beckon him back. If he waited, she would call him. He walked round the corner and heard her voice, a hundred voices, and all hers, calling his name, and a hundred names that were all his, over the bushy walls.

And what shall the terrified prig of a love-mad young man do next? he asked his reflection silently in the distorting mirror of the empty 'Victoria' saloon. His ape-like, hanging face, with 'Bass' across the forehead, gave back a cracked sneer.

If Venus came in on a plate, said the two red, melon-slice lips, I would ask for vinegar to put on her.

She could drive my guilt out; she could smooth away my shame; why didn't I stop to talk to her? he asked.

You saw a queer tart in a park, his reflection answered, she was a child of nature, oh my! oh my! Did you see the dewdrops in her hair? Stop talking to the mirror like a man in a magazine, I know you too well.

A new head, swollen and lop-jawed, wagged behind his shoulder. He spun round, to hear the barman say:

'Has the one and only let you down? You look like death warmed up. Have this one on the house. Free beer to-day. Free X's.' He pulled the beer handle. 'Only the best served here. Straight from the rust. You do look queer,' he said, 'the only one saved from the wreck and the only wreck saved. Here's looking at you!' He drank the beer he had drawn.

'May I have a glass of beer, please?'

'What do you think this is, a public house?'

On the polished table in the middle of the saloon the young man drew, with a finger dipped in strong, the round head of a girl and piled a yellow froth of hair upon it.

'Ah! dirty, dirty!' said the barman, running round from behind the counter and rubbing the head away with a dry cloth.

Shielding the dirtiness with his hat, the young man wrote his name on the edge of the table and watched the letters dry and fade.

Through the open bay-window, across the useless railway covered with sand, he saw the black dots of bathers, the stunted huts, the jumping dwarfs round the Punch and Judy, and the tiny religious circle. Since he had walked and played down there in the crowded wilderness, excusing his despair, searching for company though he refused it, he had found his own true happiness and lost her all in one bewildering and clumsy half a minute by the 'Gentlemen' and the flower clock. Older and wiser and no better, he would have looked in the mirror to see if his discovery and loss had marked themselves upon his face in shadows under the eyes or lines about the mouth, were it not for the answer he knew he would receive from the distorted reflection.

The barman came to sit near him, and said in a false voice: 'Now you tell me all about it, I'm a regular storehouse of secrets.'

'There isn't anything to tell. I saw a girl in Victoria Gardens and I was too shy to speak to her. She was a piece of God help us all right.'

Ashamed of his wish to be companionable, even in the depth of love and distress, with her calm face before his eyes and her smile reproving and forgiving him as he spoke, the young man defiled his girl on the bench, dragged her down into the spit and sawdust and dolled her up to make the barman say:

'I like them big myself. Once round Bessy, once round the gas-works. I missed the chance of a lifetime, too. Fifty lovelies in the rude and I'd left my Bunsen burner home.'

'Give me the same, please.'

'You mean similar.'

The barman drew a glass of beer, drank it, and drew another.

'I always have one with the customers,' he said, 'it puts us on even terms. Now we're just two heart-broken bachelors together.' He sat down again.

'You can't tell me anything I don't know,' he said. 'I've seen over twenty chorines from the Empire in this bar, drunk as printers. Oh, les girls! les limbs!'

'Will they be in to-night?'

'There's only a fellow sawing a woman in half this week.'

'Keep a half for me.'

A drunk man walked in on an invisible white line, and the barman, reeling in sympathy across the room, served him with a pint. 'Free beer to-day,' he said. 'Free X's. You've been out in the sun.'

'I've been out in the sun all day,' said the man.

'I thought you looked sunburnt.'

'That's drink,' said the man. 'I've been drinking.'

'The holiday is drawing to an end,' the young man whispered into his glass. Bye-bye blackbird, the moment is lost, he thought, examining, with an interest he could not forgive, the comic coloured postcards of mountain-buttocked women on the beach and hen-pecked, pin-legged men with telescopes, pasted on the wall beneath the picture of a terrier drinking stout; and now, with a jolly barman and a drunk in a crushed cap, he was mopping the failing day down. He tipped his hat over his forehead, and a lock of hair that fell below the hat tickled his eyelid. He saw, with a stranger's darting eye that missed no single subtlety of the wry grin or the faintest gesture drawing the shape of his death on the air, an unruly-haired young man who coughed into his hand in the corner of a rotting room and puffed the smoke of his doped Weight.

But as the drunk man weaved towards him on wilful feet, carrying his dignity as a man might carry a full glass around a quaking ship, as the barman behind the counter clattered and whistled and dipped to drink, he shook off the truthless, secret tragedy with a sneer and a blush, straightened his melancholy hat into a hard-brimmed trilby, dismissed the affected stranger. In the safe centre of his own identity, the familiar world about him like another flesh, he sat sad and content in the plain room of the undistinguished hotel at the sea-end of the shabby, spreading town where everything was happening. He had no need of the dark interior world when Tawe pressed in upon him and the eccentric ordinary people came bursting and crawling, with noise and colours, out of their houses, out of the graceless buildings, the factories and avenues, the shining shops and blaspheming chapels, the terminuses and the meeting-halls, the falling alleys and brick lanes, from the arches and shelters and holes behind the hoardings, out of the common, wild intelligence of the town.

At last the drunk man had reached him. 'Put your hand here,' he said, and turned about and tapped himself on the bottom.

The barman whistled and rose from his drink to see the young man touch the drunk man on the seat of the trousers.

'What can you feel there?'

'Nothing.'

'That's right. Nothing. Nothing. There's nothing there to feel.'

'How can you sit down then?' asked the barman.

'I just sit down on what the doctor left,' the man said angrily. 'I had as good a bottom as you've got once. I was working underground in Dowlais, and the end of the world came down on me. Do you know what I got for losing my bottom? Four and three! Two and three ha'pence a cheek. That's cheaper than a pig.'

The girl from Victoria Gardens came into the bar with two friends: a blonde young girl almost as beautiful as she was, and a middle-aged woman dressed and made up to look young. The three of them sat at the table. The girl he loved ordered three ports and gins.

'Isn't it delicious weather?' said the middle-aged woman.

The barman said: 'Plenty of sky about.' With many bows and smiles he placed their drinks in front of them. 'I thought the princesses had gone to a better pub,' he said.

'What's a better pub without you, handsome?' said the blonde girl.

'This is the "Ritz" and the "Savoy," isn't it, *garçon* darling?' the girl from the Gardens said, and kissed her hand to him.

The young man in the window seat, still bewildered by the first sudden sight of her entering the darkening room, caught the kiss to himself and blushed. He thought to run out of the room and through the miracle-making Gardens, to rush into his house and hide his head in the bed-clothes and lie all night there, dressed and trembling, her voice in his ears, her green eyes wide awake under his closed eyelids. But only a sick boy with tossed blood would run from his proper love into a dream, lie down in a bedroom that was full of his shames, and sob against the feathery, fat breast and face of the damp pillow. He remembered his age and poems, and would not move.

'Tanks a million, Lou,' said the barman.

Her name was Lou, Louise, Louisa. She must be Spanish or French or a gipsy, but he could tell the street that her voice came from; he knew where her friends lived by the rise and fall of their sharp voices, and the name of the middle-aged woman was Mrs Emerald Franklin. She was to be seen every night in the 'Jew's Harp,' sipping and spying and watching the clock.

'We've been listening to Matthews Hell-fire on the sands. Down with this and down with that, and he used to drink a pint of biddy before his breakfast,' Mrs Franklin said. 'Oh, there's a nerve!'

'And his eye on the fluff all the time,' said the blonde girl. 'I wouldn't trust him any further than Ramon Navarro behind the counter.'

'Whoops! I've gone up in the world. Last week I was Charley Chase,' said the barman.

Mrs Franklin raised her empty glass in a gloved hand and shook it like a bell. 'Men are deceivers ever,' she said. 'And a drop of mother's ruin right around.'

'Especially Mr Franklin,' said the barman.

'But there's a lot in what the preacher says, mind,' Mrs Franklin said, 'about the carrying on. If you go for a constitutional after stop-tap along the sands you might as well be in Sodom and Gomorrah.'

The blonde girl laughed. 'Hark to Mrs Grundy! I see her with a black man last Wednesday, round by the museum.'

'He was an Indian,' said Mrs Franklin, 'from the university college, and I'd thank you to remember it. Every one's brothers under the skin, but there's no tarbrush in my family.'

'Oh, dear! oh, dear!' said Lou. 'Lay off it, there's loves. This is my birthday. It's a holiday. Put a bit of fun in it. Miaow! miaow! Marjorie, kiss Emerald and be friends.' She smiled and laughed at them both. She winked at the barman, who was filling their glasses to the top. 'Here's to your blue eyes, *garçon*!' She had not noticed the young man in the corner. 'And one for grand-dad there,' she said, smiling at the swaying, drunk man. 'He's twenty-one to-day. There! I've made him smile.'

The drunk man made a deep, dangerous bow, lifted his hat, stumbled against the mantelpiece, and his full pint in his free hand was steady as a rock. 'The prettiest girl in Carmarthenshire,' he said.

'This is Glamorganshire, dad,' she said, 'where's your geography? Look at him waltzing! mind your glasses! He's got that Kruschen feeling. Come on, faster! give us the Charleston.'

The drunk man, with his pint held high, danced until he fell, and all the time he never spilt a drop. He lay at Lou's feet on the dusty floor and grinned up at her in confidence and affection. 'I fell,' he said. 'I could dance like a trooper when I had a beatyem.'

'He lost his bottom at the last trump,' the barman explained.

'When did he lose his bottom?' said Mrs Franklin.

'When Gabriel blew his whistle down in Dowlais.'

'You're pulling my leg.'

'It's a pleasure, Mrs Em. Hoi, you! get up from the vomitorium.'

The man wagged his end like a tail, and growled at Lou's feet.

'Put your head on my foot. Be comfy. Let him lie there,' she said.

He went to sleep at once.

'I can't have drunks on the premises.'

'You know where to go then.'

'Cru-el Mrs Franklin!'

'Go on, attend to your business. Serve the young man in the corner, his tongue's hanging out.'

'Cru-el lady!'

As Mrs Franklin called attention to the young man, Lou peered shortsightedly across the saloon and saw him sitting with his back to the window.

'I'll have to get glasses,' she said.

'You'll have plenty of glasses before the night's out.'

'No, honest, Marjorie, I didn't know any one was there. I do beg your pardon, you in the corner,' she said.

The barman switched on the light. 'A bit of *lux in tenebris*.'

'Oh!' said Lou.

The young man dared not move for fear that he might break the long light of her scrutiny, the enchantment shining like a single line of light between them, or startle her into speaking; and he did not conceal the love in his eyes, for she could pierce through to it as easily as she could turn his heart in his chest and make it beat above the noises of the two friends' hurried conversation, the rattle of glasses behind the counter where the barman spat and polished and missed nothing, and the snores of the comfortable sleeper. Nothing can hurt me. Let the barman jeer. Giggle in your glass, our Em. I'm telling the world, I'm walking in clover, I'm staring at Lou like a fool, she's my girl, she's my lily. O love! O love! She's no lady, with her sing-song Tontine voice, she drinks like a deep-sea diver; but Lou, I'm yours, and Lou, you're mine. He refused to meditate on her calmness now and twist her beauty into words. She was nothing under the sun or moon but his. Unashamed and certain, he smiled at her; and, though he was prepared for all, her answering smile made his fingers tremble again, as they had trembled in the Gardens, and reddened his cheeks and drove his heart to a gallop.

'Harold, fill the young man's glass up,' Mrs Franklin said.

The barman stood still, a duster in one hand and a dripping glass in the other.

'Have you got water in your ears? Fill the young man's glass!'

The barman put the duster to his eyes. He sobbed. He wiped away the mock tears.

'I thought I was attending a *première* and this was the royal box,' he said.

'He's got water on the brain, not in his earhole,' said Marjorie.

'I dreamt it was a beautiful tragi-comedy entitled "Love at First Sight, or, Another Good Man gone wrong." Act one in a boozer by the sea.'

The two women tapped their foreheads.

Lou said, still smiling: 'Where was the second act?'

Her voice was as gentle as he had imagined it to be before her gay and nervous playing with the over-familiar barman and the inferior women. He saw her as a wise, soft girl whom no hard company could spoil, for her soft self, bare to the heart, broke through every defence of her sensual falsifiers. As he thought this, phrasing her gentleness, faithlessly running to words away from the real room and his love in the middle, he woke with a start and saw her lively body six steps from him, no calm heart dressed in a sentence, but a pretty girl, to be got and kept. He must catch hold of her fast. He got up to cross to her.

'I woke before the second act came on,' said the barman. 'I'd sell my dear old mother to see that. Dim lights. Purple couches. Ecstatic bliss. Là, la chérie!'

The young man sat down at the table, next to her.

Harold, the barman, leaned over the counter and cupped his hand to his ear.

The man on the floor rolled in his sleep, and his head lay in the spittoon.

'You should have come and sat here a long time ago,' Lou whispered. 'You should have stopped to talk to me in the Gardens. Were you shy?'

'I was too shy,' the young man whispered.

'Whispering isn't manners. I can't hear a word,' said the barman.

At a sign from the young man, a flick of the fingers that sent the waiters in evening dress bustling with oysters about the immense room, the barman filled the glasses with port, gin, and Nutbrown.

'We never drink with strangers,' Mrs Franklin said, laughing.

'He isn't a stranger,' said Lou, 'are you, Jack?'

He threw a pound note on the table: 'Take the damage.'

The evening that had been over before it began raced along among the laughter of the charming women sharp as knives, and the stories of the barman, who should be on the stage, and Lou's delighted smiles and silences at his side. Now she is safe and sure, he thought, after her walking, like my doubtful walking, around the lonely distances of the holiday. In the warm, spinning middle they were close and alike. The town and the sea and the last pleasure-makers drifted into the dark that had nothing to do with them, and left this one room burning.

One by one, some lost men from the dark shuffled into the bar, drank sadly, and went out. Mrs Franklin, flushed and dribbling, waved her glass at their departures. Harold winked behind their backs. Marjorie showed them her long, white legs.

'Nobody loves us except ourselves,' said Harold. 'Shall I shut the bar and keep the riff-raff out?'

'Lou is expecting Mr O'Brien, but don't let that stop you,' Marjorie said. 'He's her sugar daddy from old Ireland.'

'Do you love Mr O'Brien?' the young man whispered.

'How could I, Jack?'

He could see Mr O'Brien as a witty, tall fellow of middle age, with waved greying hair and a clipped bit of dirt on his upper lip, a flash ring on his marriage finger, a pouched, knowing eye, dummy dressed with a whale-boned waist, a broth of a man about Cardiff, Lou's horrible lover tearing towards her now down the airless streets in the firm's car. The young man clenched his hand on the table covered with dead, and sheltered her in the warm strength of his fist. 'My round, my round,' he said, 'up again, plenty! Doubles, trebles, Mrs Franklin is a jibber.'

'My mother never had a jibber.'

'Oh, Lou!' he said, 'I am more than happy with you.'

'Coo! coo! hear the turtle doves.'

'Let them coo,' said Marjorie. 'I could coo, too.'

The barman looked around him in surprise. He raised his hands, palms up, and cocked his head.

'The bar is full of birds,' he said.

'Emerald's laying an egg,' he said, as Mrs Franklin rocked in her chair.

Soon the bar was full of customers. The drunk man woke up and ran out, leaving his cap in a brown pool. Sawdust dropped from his hair. A small, old, round, red-faced, cheery man sat facing the young man and Lou, who held hands under the table and rubbed their legs against each other.

'What a night for love!' said the old man. 'On such a night as this did Jessica steal from the wealthy Jew. Do you know where that comes from?'

'*The Merchant of Venice*,' Lou said. 'But you're an Irishman, Mr O'Brien.'

'I could have sworn you were a tall man with a little tish,' said the young man gravely.

'What's the weapons, Mr O'Brien?'

'Brandies at dawn, I should think, Mrs Franklin.'

'I never described Mr O'Brien to you at all. You're dreaming!' Lou whispered. 'I wish this night could go on for ever.'

'But not here. Not in the bar. In a room with a big bed.'

'A bed in a bar,' said the old man, 'if you'll pardon me hearing you, that's what I've always wanted. Think of it, Mrs Franklin.'

The barman bobbed up from behind the counter.

'Time, gentlemen and others!'

The sober strangers departed to Mrs Franklin's laughter.

The lights went out.

'Lou, don't you lose me.'

'I've got your hand.'

'Press it hard, hurt it.'

'Break his bloody neck,' Mrs Franklin said in the dark. 'No offence meant.'

'Marjorie smack hand,' said Marjorie. 'Let's get out of the dark. Harold's a rover in the dark.'

'And the girl guides.'

'Let's take a bottle each and go down to Lou's,' she said.

'I'll buy the bottles,' said Mr O'Brien.

'It's you don't lose me now,' Lou whispered. 'Hold on to me, Jack. The others won't stay long. Oh, Mr Christ, I wish it was just you and me!'

'Will it be just you and me?'

'You and me and Mr Moon.'

Mr O'Brien opened the saloon door. 'Pile into the Rolls, you ladies. The gentlemen are going to see to the medicine.'

The young man felt Lou's quick kiss on his mouth before she followed Marjorie and Mrs Franklin out.

'What do you say we split the drinks?' said Mr O'Brien.

'Look what I found in the lavatory,' said the barman, 'he was singing on the seat.' He appeared behind the counter with the drunk man leaning on his arm.

They all climbed into the car.

'First stop, Lou's.'

The young man, on Lou's knee, saw the town in a daze spin by them, the funnelled and masted smoke-blue outline of the still, droning docks, the lightning lines of the poor streets growing longer, and the winking shops that were snapped out one by one. The car smelt of scent and powder and flesh. He struck with his elbow, by accident, Mrs Franklin's upholstered breast. Her thighs, like cushions, bore the drunk man's rolling weight. He was bumped and tossed on a lump of women. Breasts, legs, bellies, hands, touched, warmed, and smothered him. On through the night, towards Lou's bed, towards the unbelievable end of the dying holiday, they tore past black houses and bridges, a station in a smoke cloud, and drove up a steep side street with one weak lamp in a circle of railings at the top, and swerved into a space where a tall tenement house stood surrounded by cranes, standing ladders, poles and girders, barrows, brick-heaps.

They climbed to Lou's room up many flights of dark, perilous stairs. Washing hung on the rails outside closed doors. Mrs Franklin, fumbling alone with the drunk man behind the others, trod in a bucket, and a lucky black cat ran over her foot. Lou led the young man by the hand through a passage marked with names and doors, lit a match, and whispered: 'It won't be very long. Be good and patient with Mr

O'Brien. Here it is. Come in first. Welcome to you, Jack!' She kissed him again at the door of her home. 'That kiss is my promise.'

She turned on the light, and he walked with her proudly into her own room, into the room that he would come to know, and saw a wide bed, a gramophone on a chair, a wash-basin half-hidden in a corner, a gas fire and a cooking ring, a closed cupboard, and her photograph in a cardboard frame on the chest of drawers with no handles. Here she slept and ate. In the double bed she lay all night, pale and curled, sleeping on her left side. When he lived with her always, he would not allow her to dream. No other men must lie and love in her head. He spread his fingers on her pillow.

'Why do you live at the top of the Eiffel Tower?' said the barman, coming in.

'What a climb!' said Mr O'Brien. 'But it's very nice and private when you get here.'

'If you get here!' said Mrs Franklin. 'I'm dead beat. This old nuisance weighs a ton. Lie down, lie down on the floor and go to sleep. The old nuisance!' she said fondly. 'What's your name?'

'Ernie,' the drunk man said, raising his arm to shield his face.

'Nobody's going to bite you, Ernie. Here, give him a nip of whisky. Careful! Don't pour it on your waistcoat; you'll be squeezing your waistcoat in the morning. Pull the curtains, Lou, I can see the wicked old moon,' she said.

'Does it put ideas in your head?'

'I love the moon,' said Lou.

'There never was a young lover who didn't love the moon.' Mr O'Brien gave the young man a cheery smile, and patted his hand. His own hand was red and hairy. 'I could see at the flash of a glance that Lou and this nice young fellow were made for each other. I could see it in their eyes. Dear me, no! I'm not so old and blind I can't see love in front of my nose. Couldn't you see it, Mrs Franklin? Couldn't you see it, Marjorie?'

In the long silence, Lou collected glasses from the cupboard as though she had not heard Mr O'Brien speak. She drew the curtains, shut out the moon, sat on the edge of her bed with her feet tucked under her, looked at her photograph as at a stranger, folded her hands as she had folded them, on the first meeting, before the young man's worship in the Gardens.

'A host of angels must be passing by,' said Mr O'Brien. 'What a silence there is! Have I said anything out of place? Drink and be merry, to-morrow we die. What do you think I bought these lovely shining bottles for?'

The bottles were opened. The dead were lined on the mantelpiece. The whisky went down. Harold the barman and Marjorie, her dress lifted, sat in the one arm-chair together. Mrs Franklin, with Ernie's head on her lap, sang in a sweet, trained contralto voice *The Shepherd's Lass*. Mr O'Brien kept rhythm with his foot.

I want Lou in my arms, the young man said to himself, watching Mr O'Brien tap and smile and the barman draw Marjorie down deep. Mrs Franklin's voice sang sweetly in the small bedroom where he and Lou should be lying in the white bed without any smiling company to see them drown. He and Lou could go down together, one cool body weighted with a boiling stone, on to the falling, blank white, entirely empty sea, and never rise. Sitting on their bridal bed, near enough to hear his breath, she was farther from him than before they met. Then he had everything but her body; now she had given him two kisses, and everything had vanished but that beginning. He must be good and patient with Mr O'Brien. He could wipe away the embracing, old smile with the iron back of his hand. Sink lower, lower, Harold and Marjorie, tumble like whales at Mr O'Brien's feet.

He wished that the light would fail. In the darkness he and Lou could creep beneath the clothes and imitate the dead. Who would look for them there, if they were dead still and soundless? The others would shout to them down the dizzy stairs or rummage in the silence about the narrow, obstacled corridors or stumble out into the night to search for them among the cranes and ladders in the desolation of the destroyed houses. He could hear, in the made-up dark, Mr O'Brien's voice cry, 'Lou, where are you? Answer! answer!' the hollow answer of the echo, 'answer!' and hear her lips in the cool pit of the bed secretly move around another name, and feel them move,

'A fine piece of singing, Emerald, and very naughty words. That was a shepherd, that was,' Mr O'Brien said.

Ernie, on the floor, began to sing in a thick, sulking voice, but Mrs Franklin placed her hand over his mouth and he sucked and nuzzled it.

'What about this young shepherd?' said Mr O'Brien, pointing his glass at the young man. 'Can he sing as well as make love? You ask him kindly, girlie,' he said to Lou, 'and he'll give us a song like a nightingale.'

'Can you sing, Jack?'

'Like a crow, Lou.'

'Can't he even talk poetry? What a young man to have who can't spout the poets to his lady!' Mr O'Brien said.

From the cupboard Lou brought out a red-bound book and gave it to the young man, saying: 'Can you read us a piece out of here? The second volume's in the hat-box. Read us a dreamy piece, Jack. It's nearly midnight.'

'Only a love poem, no other kind,' said Mr O'Brien. 'I won't hear anything but a love poem.'

'Soft and sweet,' Mrs Franklin said. She took her hand away from Ernie's mouth and looked at the ceiling.

The young man read, but not aloud, lingering on her name, the inscription on the fly-leaf of the first volume of the collected poems of Tennyson: 'To Louisa, from her Sunday School teacher, Miss Gwyneth Forbes. God's in His Heaven, all's right with the world.'

'Make it a love poem, don't forget.'

The young man read aloud, closing one eye to steady the dancing print, *Come into the Garden, Maud*. And when he reached the beginning of the fourth verse his voice grew louder:

'I said to the lily, "There is but one
With whom she has heart to be gay.
When will the dancers leave her alone?
She is weary of dance and play."
Now half to the setting moon are gone,
And half to the rising day;
Low on the sand and loud on the stone
The last wheel echoes away.
'I said to the rose, "The brief night goes
In babble and revel and wine.
O young lord-lover, what sighs are those,
For one that will never be thine?
But mine, but mine," so I sware to the rose,
"For ever and ever, mine."'

At the end of the poem, Harold said, suddenly, his head hanging over the arm of the chair, his hair made wild, and his mouth red with lipstick: 'My grandfather remembers seeing Lord Tennyson, he was a little man with a hump.'

'No,' said the young man, 'he was tall and he had long hair and a beard.'

'Did you ever see him?'

'I wasn't born then.'

'My grandfather saw him. He had a hump.'

'Not Alfred Tennyson.'

'Lord Alfred Tennyson was a little man with a hump.'

'It couldn't have been the same Tennyson.'

'You've got the wrong Tennyson, this was the famous poet with a hump.'

Lou, on the wonderful bed, waiting for him alone of all the men, ugly or handsome, old or young, in the wide town and the small world that would be bound to fall, lowered her head and kissed her hand to him and held her hand in the river of light on the counterpane. The hand, to him, became transparent, and the light on the counterpane glowed up steadily through it in the thin shape of her palm and fingers.

'Ask Mr O'Brien what Lord Tennyson was like,' said Mrs Franklin. 'We appeal to you, Mr O'Brien, did he have a hump or not?'

Nobody but the young man, for whom she lived and waited now, noticed Lou's little loving movements. She put her glowing hand to her left breast. She made a sign of secrecy on her lips.

'It depends,' Mr O'Brien said.

The young man closed one eye again, for the bed was pitching like a ship; a sickening, hot storm out of a cigarette cloud unsettled cupboard and chest. The motions of the sea-going bedroom were calmed with the cunning closing of his eye, but he longed for night air. On sailor's legs he walked to the door.

'You'll find the House of Commons on the second floor at the end of the passage,' said Mr O'Brien.

At the door, he turned to Lou and smiled with all his love, declaring it to the faces of the company and making her, before Mr O'Brien's envious regard, smile back and say: 'Don't be long, Jack. Please! You mustn't be long.'

Now every one knew. Love had grown up in an evening.

'One minute, my darling,' he said. 'I'll be here.'

The door closed behind him. He walked into the wall of the passage. He lit a match. He had three left. Down the stairs, clinging to the sticky, shaking rails, rocking on see-saw floorboards, bruising his shin on a bucket, past the noises of secret lives behind doors he slid and stumbled and swore and heard Lou's voice in a fresh fever drive him on, call him to return, speak to him with such passion and abandonment that even in the darkness and the pain of his haste he was dazzled and struck still. She spoke, there on the rotting stairs in the middle of the poor house, a frightening rush of love words; from her mouth, at his ear, endearments were burned out. Hurry! hurry! Every moment is being killed. Love, adored, dear, run back and whistle to me, open the door, shout my name, lay me down. Mr O'Brien has his hands on my side.

He ran into a cavern. A draught blew out his matches. He lurched into a room where two figures on a black heap on the floor lay whispering, and ran from there in a panic. He made water at the dead end of the passage and hurried back towards Lou's room, finding himself at last on a silent patch of stairway at the top of the house; he put out his hand, but the rail was broken and nothing there prevented a long drop to the ground down a twisted shaft that would echo and double his cry, bring out from their holes in the wall the sleeping or stirring families, the whispering figures, the blind startled turners of night into day. Lost in a tunnel near the roof, he fingered the damp walls for a door; he found a handle and gripped it hard, but it came off in his hand. Lou had led him down a longer passage than this. He remembered the number of doors: there were three on each side. He ran down the broken-railed flight into another passage and dragged his hand along the wall. Three doors, he counted. He opened the third door, walked into darkness, and groped for the switch on the left. He saw, in the sudden light, a bed and a cupboard and a chest of drawers with no handles, a gas fire, a wash-basin in the corner. No bottles. No glasses. No photograph of Lou. The red counterpane on the bed was smooth. He could not remember the colour of Lou's counterpane.

He left the light burning and opened the second door, but a strange woman's voice cried, half-asleep: 'Who is there? Is it you, Tom? Tom, put the light on.' He looked for a line of light at the foot of the next door, and stopped to listen for voices. The woman was still calling in the second room.

'Lou, where are you?' he cried. 'Answer! answer!'

'Lou, what Lou? There's no Lou here,' said a man's voice through the open door of the first dark room at the entrance to the passage.

He scampered down another flight and counted four doors with his scratched hand. One door opened and a woman in a nightdress put out her head. A child's head appeared below her.

'Where does Lou live? Do you know where Lou lives?'

The woman and the child stared without speaking.

'Lou! Lou! her name is Lou!' he heard himself shout. 'She lives here, in this house! Do you know where she lives?'

The woman caught the child by the hair and pulled her into the room. He clung to the edge of her door. The woman thrust her arm round the edge and brought down a bunch of keys sharply on his hands. The door slammed.

A young woman with a baby in a shawl stood at an open door on the opposite side of the passage, and caught his sleeve as he ran by. 'Lou who? You woke my baby.'

'I don't know her other name. She's with Mrs Franklin and Mr O'Brien.'

'You woke my baby.'

'Come in and find her in the bed,' a voice said from the darkness behind the young woman.

'He's woken up the baby.'

He ran down the passage, holding his wet hand to his mouth. He fell against the rails of the last flight of stairs. He heard Lou's voice in his head once more whisper to him to return as the ground floor rose, like a lift full of dead, towards the rails. Hurry! hurry! I can't, I won't wait, the bridal night is being killed.

Up the rotten, bruising, mountainous stairs he climbed, in his sickness, to the passage where he had left the one light burning in an end room. The light was out. He tapped all the doors and whispered her name. He beat on the doors and shouted, and a woman, dressed in a vest and a hat, drove him out of the passage with a walking-stick.

For a long time he waited on the stairs, though there was no love now to wait for and no bed but his own too many miles away to lie in, and only the approaching day to remember his discovery. All around him the disturbed inhabitants of the house were falling back into sleep. Then he walked out of the house on to the waste space and under the leaning cranes and ladders. The light of the one weak lamp in a rusty circle fell across the brick-heaps and the broken wood and the dust that had been houses once, where the small and hardly known and never-to-be-forgotten people of the dirty town had lived and loved and died and, always, lost.

Under Milk Wood

[*Silence*]

FIRST VOICE (*Very softly*)
To begin at the beginning:

It is Spring, moonless night in the small town, starless and bible-black, the cobblestreets silent and the hunched, courters'-and-rabbits' wood limping invisible down to the sloeblack, slow, black, crowblack, fishingboat-bobbing sea. The houses are blind as moles (though moles see fine to-night in the snouting, velvet dingles) or blind as Captain Cat there in the muffled middle by the pump and the town clock, the shops in mourning, the Welfare Hall in widows' weeds. And all the people of the lulled and dumbfound town are sleeping now.

Hush, the babies are sleeping, the farmers, the fishers, the tradesmen and pensioners, cobbler, schoolteacher, postman and publican, the undertaker and the fancy woman, drunkard, dressmaker, preacher, policeman, the webfoot cocklewomen and the tidy wives. Young girls lie bedded soft or glide in their dreams, with rings and trousseaux, bridesmaided by glow-worms down the aisles of the organplaying wood. The boys are dreaming wicked or of the bucking ranches of the night and the jollyrodgered sea. And the anthracite statues of the horses sleep in the fields, and the cows in the byres, and the dogs in the wet-nosed yards; and the cats nap in the slant corners or lope sly, streaking and needling, on the one cloud of the roofs.

You can hear the dew falling, and the hushed town breathing.

Only *your* eyes are unclosed to see the black and folded town fast, and slow, asleep. And you alone can hear the invisible starfall, the darkest-before-dawn minutely dewgrazed stir of the black, dab-filled sea where the *Arethusa*, the *Curlew* and the *Skylark*, *Zanzibar*, *Rhiannon*, the *Rover*, the *Cormorant*, and the *Star of Wales* tilt and ride.

Listen. It is night moving in the streets, the processional salt slow musical wind in Coronation Street and Cockle Row, it is the grass growing on Llareggub Hill, dewfall, starfall, the sleep of birds in Milk Wood.

Listen. It is night in the chill, squat chapel, hymning in bonnet and brooch and bombazine black, butterfly choker and bootlace bow, coughing like nannygoats, sucking mintoes, fortywinking hallelujah; night in the four-ale, quiet as a domino; in Ocky Milkman's lofts like a mouse with gloves; in Dai Bread's bakery flying like black flour. It is to-night in Donkey Street, trotting silent, with seaweed on its hooves, along the cockled cobbles, past curtained fernpot, text and trinket, harmonium, holy dresser, watercolours done by hand, china dog and rosy tin teacaddy. It is night neddying among the snuggeries of babies.

Look. It is night, dumbly, royally winding through the Coronation cherry trees; going through the graveyard of Bethesda with winds gloved and folded, and dew doffed; tumbling by the Sailors Arms.

Time passes. Listen. Time passes.

Come closer now.

Only you can hear the houses sleeping in the streets in the slow deep salt and silent black, bandaged night. Only you can see, in the blinded bedrooms, the combs and petticoats over the chairs, the jugs and basins, the glasses of teeth, Thou Shalt Not on the wall, and the yellowing dickybird-watching pictures of the dead. Only you can hear and see, behind the eyes of the sleepers, the movements and countries and mazes and colours and dismays and rainbows and tunes and wishes and flight and fall and despairs and big seas of their dreams.

From where you are, you can hear their dreams.

Captain Cat, the retired blind seacaptain, asleep in his bunk in the seashelled, ship-in-bottled, shipshape best cabin of Schooner House dreams of

SECOND VOICE

never such seas as any that swamped the decks of his S.S. *Kidwelly* bellying over the bedclothes and jellyfish-slippery sucking him down salt deep into the Davy dark where the fish come biting out and nibble him down to his wishbone, and the long drowned nuzzle up to him.

FIRST DROWNED
Remember me, Captain?
CAPTAIN CAT
You're Dancing Williams!
FIRST DROWNED
I lost my step in Nantucket.
SECOND DROWNED
Do you see me, Captain? the white bone talking? I'm Tom-Fred the donkeyman... we shared the same girl once... her name was Mrs Probert...
WOMAN'S VOICE
Rosie Probert, thirty three Duck Lane. Come on up, boys, I'm dead.
THIRD DROWNED
Hold me, Captain, I'm Jonah Jarvis, come to a bad end, very enjoyable.
FOURTH DROWNED
Alfred Pomeroy Jones, sealawyer, born in Mumbles, sung like a linnet, crowned you with a flagon, tattooed with mermaids, thirst like a dredger, died of blisters.
FIRST DROWNED
This skull at your earhole is
FIFTH DROWNED
Curly Bevan. Tell my auntie it was me that pawned the ormolu clock.
CAPTAIN CAT
Aye, aye, Curly.
SECOND DROWNED
Tell my missus no I never
THIRD DROWNED

I never done what she said I never
FOURTH DROWNED
Yes, they did.
FIFTH DROWNED
And who brings coconuts and shawls and parrots to *my* Gwen now?
FIRST DROWNED
How's it above?
SECOND DROWNED
Is there rum and lavabread?
THIRD DROWNED
Bosoms and robins?
FOURTH DROWNED
Concertinas?
FIFTH DROWNED
Ebenezer's bell?
FIRST DROWNED
Fighting and onions?
SECOND DROWNED
And sparrows and daisies?
THIRD DROWNED
Tiddlers in a jamjar?
FOURTH DROWNED
Buttermilk and whippets?
FIFTH DROWNED
Rock-a-bye baby?
FIRST DROWNED
Washing on the line?
SECOND DROWNED
And old girls in the snug?
THIRD DROWNED
How's the tenors in Dowlais?

FOURTH DROWNED
Who milks the cows in Maesgwyn?
FIFTH DROWNED
When she smiles, is there dimples?
FIRST DROWNED
What's the smell of parsley?
CAPTAIN CAT
Oh, my dead dears!
FIRST VOICE
From where you are, you can hear in Cockle Row in the spring, moonless night, Miss Price, dressmaker and sweetshop-keeper, dream of
SECOND VOICE
her lover, tall as the town clock tower, Samson-syrup-gold-maned, whacking thighed and piping hot, thunderbolt-bass'd and barnacle-breasted, flailing up the cockles with his eyes like blowlamps and scooping low over her lonely loving hotwaterbottled body.
MR EDWARDS
Myfanwy Price!
MISS PRICE
Mr Mog Edwards!
MR EDWARDS
I am a draper mad with love. I love you more than all the flannelette and calico, candlewick, dimity, crash and merino, tussore, cretonne, crépon, muslin, poplin, ticking and twill in the whole Cloth Hall of the world. I have come to take you away to my Emporium on the hill, where the change hums on wires. Throw away your little bedsocks and your Welsh wool knitted jacket, I will warm the sheets like an electric toaster, I will lie by your side like the Sunday roast.
MISS PRICE

I will knit you a wallet of forget-me-not blue, for the money to be comfy. I will warm your heart by the fire so that you can slip it in under your vest when the shop is closed.

MR EDWARDS

Myfanwy, Myfanwy, before the mice gnaw at your bottom drawer will you say

MISS PRICE

Yes, Mog, yes, Mog, yes, yes, yes.

MR EDWARDS

And all the bells of the tills of the town shall ring for our wedding.

[*Noise of money-tills and chapel bells*

FIRST VOICE

Come now, drift up the dark, come up the drifting sea-dark street now in the dark night seesawing like the sea, to the bible-black airless attic over Jack Black the cobbler's shop where alone and savagely Jack Black sleeps in a nightshirt tied to his ankles with elastic and dreams of

SECOND VOICE

chasing the naughty couples down the grassgreen gooseberried double bed of the wood, flogging the tosspots in the spit-and-sawdust, driving out the bare bold girls from the sixpenny hops of his nightmares.

JACK BLACK (*Loudly*)

Ach y fi!

Ach y fi!

FIRST VOICE

Evans the Death, the undertaker,

SECOND VOICE

laughs high and aloud in his sleep and curls up his toes as he sees, upon waking fifty years ago, snow lie deep on the goosefield behind the sleeping house; and he runs out into the field where his mother is making welshcakes in the snow, and steals a fistful of snowflakes and currants and climbs back to bed to eat them cold and sweet under the

warm, white clothes while his mother dances in the snow kitchen crying out for her lost currants.
FIRST VOICE
And in the little pink-eyed cottage next to the undertaker's, lie, alone, the seventeen snoring gentle stone of Mister Waldo, rabbitcatcher, barber, herbalist, catdoctor, quack, his fat pink hands, palms up, over the edge of the patchwork quilt, his black boots neat and tidy in the washing-basin, his bowler on a nail above the bed, a milk stout and a slice of cold bread pudding under the pillow; and, dripping in the dark, he dreams of
MOTHER
This little piggy went to market
This little piggy stayed at home
This little piggy had roast beef
This little piggy had none
And this little piggy went
LITTLE BOY
wee wee wee wee wee
MOTHER
all the way home to
WIFE (*Screaming*)
Waldo! Wal-do!
MR WALDO
Yes, Blodwen love?
WIFE
Oh, what'll the neighbours say, what'll the neighbours . . .
FIRST NEIGHBOUR
Poor Mrs Waldo
SECOND NEIGHBOUR
What she puts up with
FIRST NEIGHBOUR
Never should of married

SECOND NEIGHBOUR
If she didn't had to
FIRST NEIGHBOUR
Same as her mother
SECOND NEIGHBOUR
There's a husband for you
FIRST NEIGHBOUR
Bad as his father
SECOND NEIGHBOUR
And you know where he ended
FIRST NEIGHBOUR
Up in the asylum
SECOND NEIGHBOUR
Crying for his ma
FIRST NEIGHBOUR
Every Saturday
SECOND NEIGHBOUR
He hasn't got a leg
FIRST NEIGHBOUR
And carrying on
SECOND NEIGHBOUR
With that Mrs Beattie Morris
FIRST NEIGHBOUR
Up in the quarry
SECOND NEIGHBOUR
And seen her baby
FIRST NEIGHBOUR
It's got his nose
SECOND NEIGHBOUR
Oh, it makes my heart bleed
FIRST NEIGHBOUR
What he'll do for drink

SECOND NEIGHBOUR
He sold the pianola
FIRST NEIGHBOUR
And her sewing machine
SECOND NEIGHBOUR
Falling in the gutter
FIRST NEIGHBOUR
Talking to the lamp-post
SECOND NEIGHBOUR
Using language
FIRST NEIGHBOUR
Singing in the w.
SECOND NEIGHBOUR
Poor Mrs Waldo
WIFE (*Tearfully*)
... Oh, Waldo, Waldo!
MR WALDO
Hush, love, hush. I'm *widower* Waldo now.
MOTHER (*Screaming*)
Waldo, Wal-do!
LITTLE BOY
Yes, our mum?
MOTHER
Oh, what'll the neighbours say, what'll the neighbours ...
THIRD NEIGHBOUR
Black as a chimbley
FOURTH NEIGHBOUR
Ringing doorbells
THIRD NEIGHBOUR
Breaking windows
FOURTH NEIGHBOUR
Making mudpies

THIRD NEIGHBOUR
Stealing currants
FOURTH NEIGHBOUR
Chalking words
THIRD NEIGHBOUR
Saw him in the bushes
FOURTH NEIGHBOUR
Playing mwchins
THIRD NEIGHBOUR
Send him to bed without any supper
FOURTH NEIGHBOUR
Give him sennapods and lock him in the dark
THIRD NEIGHBOUR
Off to the reformatory
FOURTH NEIGHBOUR
Off to the reformatory
TOGETHER
Learn him with a slipper on his b.t.m.
ANOTHER MOTHER (*Screaming*)
Waldo, Wal-do! What you doing with our Matti?
LITTLE BOY
Give us a kiss, Matti Richards.
LITTLE GIRL
Give us a penny then.
MR WALDO
I only got a halfpenny.
FIRST WOMAN
Lips is a penny.
PREACHER
Will you take this woman Matti Richards
SECOND WOMAN
Dulcie Prothero

THIRD WOMAN
Effie Bevan
FOURTH WOMAN
Lil the Gluepot
FIFTH WOMAN
Mrs Flusher
WIFE
Blodwen Bowen
PREACHER
To be your awful wedded wife
LITTLE BOY (*Screaming*)
No, no, no!
FIRST VOICE
Now, in her iceberg-white, holily laundered crinoline nightgown, under virtuous polar sheets, in her spruced and scoured dust-defying bedroom in trig and trim Bay View, a house for paying guests at the top of the town, Mrs Ogmore-Pritchard, widow, twice, of Mr Ogmore, linoleum, retired, and Mr Pritchard, failed bookmaker, who maddened by besoming, swabbing and scrubbing, the voice of the vacuum-cleaner and the fume of polish, ironically swallowed disinfectant, fidgets in her rinsed sleep, wakes in a dream, and nudges in the ribs dead Mr Ogmore, dead Mr Pritchard, ghostly on either side.
MRS OGMORE-PRITCHARD
Mr Ogmore!
Mr Pritchard!
It is time to inhale your balsam.
MR OGMORE
Oh, Mrs Ogmore!
MR PRITCHARD
Oh, Mrs Pritchard!
MRS PRITCHARD
Soon it will be time to get up.

Tell me your tasks, in order.
MR OGMORE
I must put my pyjamas in the drawer marked pyjamas.
MR PRITCHARD
I must take my cold bath which is good for me.
MR OGMORE
I must wear my flannel band to ward off sciatica.
MR PRITCHARD
I must dress behind the curtain and put on my apron.
MR OGMORE
I must blow my nose.
MRS OGMORE-PRITCHARD
In the garden, if you please.
MR OGMORE
In a piece of tissue-paper which I afterwards burn.
MR PRITCHARD
I must take my salts which are nature's friend.
MR OGMORE
I must boil the drinking water because of germs.
MR PRITCHARD
I must take my herb tea which is free from tannin.
MR OGMORE
And have a charcoal biscuit which is good for me.
MR PRITCHARD
I may smoke one pipe of asthma mixture.
MRS OGMORE-PRITCHARD
In the woodshed, if you please.
MR PRITCHARD
And dust the parlour and spray the canary.
MR OGMORE
I must put on rubber gloves and search the peke for fleas.
MR PRITCHARD

I must dust the blinds and then I must raise them.
MRS OGMORE-PRITCHARD
And before you let the sun in, mind it wipes its shoes.
FIRST VOICE
In Butcher Beynon's, Gossamer Beynon, daughter, schoolteacher, dreaming deep, daintily ferrets under a fluttering hummock of chicken's feathers in a slaughterhouse that has chintz curtains and a three-pieced suite, and finds, with no surprise, a small rough ready man with a bushy tail winking in a paper carrier.
GOSSAMER BEYNON
At last, my love,
FIRST VOICE
sighs Gossamer Beynon. And the bushy tail wags rude and ginger.
ORGAN MORGAN
Help,
SECOND VOICE
cries Organ Morgan, the organist, in his dream,
ORGAN MORGAN
there is perturbation and music in Coronation Street! All the spouses are honking like geese and the babies singing opera. P.C. Attila Rees has got his truncheon out and is playing cadenzas by the pump, the cows from Sunday Meadow ring like reindeer, and on the roof of Handel Villa see the Women's Welfare hoofing, bloomered, in the moon.
FIRST VOICE
At the sea-end of town, Mr and Mrs Floyd, the cocklers, are sleeping as quiet as death, side by wrinkled side, toothless, salt and brown, like two old kippers in a box.
And high above, in Salt Lake Farm, Mr Utah Watkins counts, all night, the wife-faced sheep as they leap the fences on the hill, smiling and knitting and bleating just like Mrs Utah Watkins.
UTAH WATKINS (*Yawning*)

Thirty-four, thirty-five, thirty-six, forty-eight, eighty-nine...
MRS UTAH WATKINS (*Bleating*)
Knit one slip one
Knit two together
Pass the slipstitch over...
FIRST VOICE
Ocky Milkman, drowned asleep in Cockle Street, is emptying his chums into the Dewi River,
OCKY MILKMAN (*Whispering*)
regardless of expense,
FIRST VOICE
and weeping like a funeral.
SECOND VOICE
Cherry Owen, next door, lifts a tankard to his lips but nothing flows out of it. He shakes the tankard. It turns into a fish. He drinks the fish.
FIRST VOICE
P.C. Attila Rees lumps out of bed, dead to the dark and still foghorning, and drags out his helmet from under the bed; but deep in the backyard lock-up of his sleep a mean voice murmurs
A VOICE (*Murmuring*)
You'll be sorry for this in the morning,
FIRST VOICE
and he heave-ho's back to bed. His helmet swashes in the dark.
SECOND VOICE
Willy Nilly, postman, asleep up street, walks fourteen miles to deliver the post as he does every day of the night, and rat-a-tats hard and sharp on Mrs Willy Nilly.
MRS WILLY NILLY
Don't spank me, please, teacher,
SECOND VOICE

whimpers his wife at his side, but every night of her married life she has been late for school.

FIRST VOICE

Sinbad Sailors, over the taproom of the Sailors Arms, hugs his damp pillow whose secret name is Gossamer Beynon.

A mogul catches Lily Smalls in the wash-house.

LILY SMALLS

Ooh, you old mogul!

SECOND VOICE

Mrs Rose Cottage's eldest, Mae, peals off her pink-and-white skin in a furnace in a tower in a cave in a waterfall in a wood and waits there raw as an onion for Mister Right to leap up the burning tall hollow splashes of leaves like a brilliantined trout.

MAE ROSE COTTAGE (*Very close and softly, drawing out the words*)

Call me Dolores

Like they do in the stories.

FIRST VOICE

Alone until she dies, Bessie Bighead, hired help, born in the workhouse, smelling of the cowshed, snores bass and gruff on a couch of straw in a loft in Salt Lake Farm and picks a posy of daisies in Sunday Meadow to put on the grave of Gomer Owen who kissed her once by the pig-sty when she wasn't looking and never kissed her again although she was looking all the time.

And the Inspectors of Cruelty fly down into Mrs Butcher Beynon's dream to persecute Mr Beynon for selling

BUTCHER BEYNON

owl meat, dogs' eyes, manchop.

SECOND VOICE

Mr Beynon, in butcher's bloodied apron, spring-heels down Coronation Street, a finger, not his own, in his mouth. Straightfaced in his cunning sleep he pulls the legs of his dreams and

BUTCHER BEYNON
ORGAN MORGAN (*High and softly*)
hunting on pigback shoots down the wild giblets.
Help!
GOSSAMER BEYNON (*Softly*)
My foxy darling.
FIRST VOICE
Now behind the eyes and secrets of the dreamers in the streets rocked to sleep by the sea, see the
SECOND VOICE
titbits and topsyturvies, bobs and buttontops, bags and bones, ash and rind and dandruff and nailparings, saliva and snowflakes and moulted feathers of dreams, the wrecks and sprats and shells and fishbones, whale-juice and moonshine and small salt fry dished up by the hidden sea.
FIRST VOICE
The owls are hunting. Look, over Bethesda gravestones one hoots and swoops and catches a mouse by Hannah Rees, Beloved Wife. And in Coronation Street, which you alone can see it is so dark under the chapel in the skies, the Reverend Eli Jenkins, poet, preacher, turns in his deep towards-dawn sleep and dreams of
REVEREND ELI JENKINS
Eisteddfodau.
SECOND VOICE
He intricately rhymes, to the music of crwth and pibgorn, all night long in his druid's seedy nightie in a beer-tent black with parchs.
FIRST VOICE
Mr Pugh, schoolmaster, fathoms asleep, pretends to be sleeping, spies foxy round the droop of his night-cap and pssst! whistles up
MR PUGH
Murder.
FIRST VOICE

Mrs Organ Morgan, groceress, coiled grey like a dormouse, her paws to her ears, conjures

MRS ORGAN MORGAN
Silence.

SECOND VOICE
She sleeps very dulcet in a cove of wool, and trumpeting Organ Morgan at her side snores no louder than a spider.

FIRST VOICE
Mary Ann Sailors dreams of

MARY ANN SAILORS
the Garden of Eden.

FIRST VOICE
She comes in her smock-frock and clogs

MARY ANN SAILORS
away from the cool scrubbed cobbled kitchen with the Sunday-school pictures on the whitewashed wall and the farmers' almanac hung above the settle and the sides of bacon on the ceiling hooks, and goes down the cockleshelled paths of that applepie kitchen garden, ducking under the gippo's clothespegs, catching her apron on the blackcurrant bushes, past bean-rows and onion-bed and tomatoes ripening on the wall towards the old man playing the harmonium in the orchard, and sits down on the grass at his side and shells the green peas that grow up through the lap of her frock that brushes the dew.

FIRST VOICE
In Donkey Street, so furred with sleep, Dai Bread, Polly Garter, Nogood Boyo, and Lord Cut-Glass sigh before the dawn that is about to be and dream of

DAI BREAD
Harems.

POLLY GARTER
Babies.

NOGOOD BOYO

Nothing.
LORD CUT-GLASS
Tick tock tick tock tick tock tick tock.
FIRST VOICE
Time passes. Listen. Time passes. An owl flies home past Bethesda, to a chapel in an oak. And the dawn inches up.
[*One distant bell-note, faintly reverberating*
FIRST VOICE
Stand on this hill. This is Llareggub Hill, old as the hills, high, cool, and green, and from this small circle of stones, made not by druids but by Mrs Beynon's Billy, you can see all the town below you sleeping in the first of the dawn.

You can hear the love-sick woodpigeons mooning in bed. A dog barks in his sleep, farmyards away. The town ripples like a lake in the waking haze.
VOICE OF A GUIDE-BOOK
Less than five hundred souls inhabit the three quaint streets and the few narrow by-lanes and scattered farmsteads that constitute this small, decaying watering-place which may, indeed, be called a 'backwater of life' without disrespect to its natives who possess, to this day, a salty individuality of their own. The main street, Coronation Street, consists, for the most part, of humble, two-storied houses many of which attempt to achieve some measure of gaiety by prinking themselves out in crude colours and by the liberal use of pinkwash, though there are remaining a few eighteenth-century houses of more pretension, if, on the whole, in a sad state of disrepair. Though there is little to attract the hillclimber, the healthseeker, the sportsman, or the weekending motorist, the contemplative may, if sufficiently attracted to spare it some leisurely hours, find, in its cobbled streets and its little fishing harbour, in its several curious customs, and in the conversation of its local 'characters,' some of that picturesque sense of the past so frequently lacking in towns and villages which have kept more abreast

of the times. The River Dewi is said to abound in trout, but is much poached. The one place of worship, with its neglected graveyard, is of no architectural interest.

[*A cock crows*
FIRST VOICE
The principality of the sky lightens now, over our green hill, into spring morning larked and crowed and belling.

[*Slow bell notes*
FIRST VOICE
Who pulls the townhall bellrope but blind Captain Cat? One by one, the sleepers are rung out of sleep this one morning as every morning. And soon you shall see the chimneys' slow upflying snow as Captain Cat, in sailor's cap and seaboots, announces to-day with his loud get-out-of-bed bell.

SECOND VOICE
The Reverend Eli Jenkins, in Bethesda House, gropes out of bed into his preacher's black, combs back his bard's white hair, forgets to wash, pads barefoot downstairs, opens the front door, stands in the doorway and, looking out at the day and up at the eternal hill, and hearing the sea break and the gab of birds, remembers his own verses and tells them softly to empty Coronation Street that is rising and raising its blinds.

REVEREND ELI JENKINS
Dear Gwalia! I know there are
Towns lovelier than ours,
And fairer hills and loftier far,
And groves more full of flowers,
And boskier woods more blithe with spring
And bright with birds' adorning,
And sweeter bards than I to sing
Their praise this beauteous morning.
By Cader Idris, tempest-torn,

Or Moel yr Wyddfa's glory,
Carnedd Llewelyn beauty born,
Plinlimmon old in story,
By mountains where King Arthur dreams,
By Penmaenmawr defiant,
Llareggub Hill a molehill seems,
A pygmy to a giant.
By Sawddwy, Senny, Dovey, Dee,
Edw, Eden, Aled, all,
Taff and Towy broad and free,
Llyfnant with its waterfall,
Claerwen, Cleddau, Dulais, Daw,
Ely, Gwili, Ogwr, Nedd,
Small is our River Dewi, Lord,
A baby on a rushy bed.
By Carreg Cennen, King of time,
Our Heron Head is only
A bit of stone with seaweed spread
Where gulls come to be lonely.
A tiny dingle is Milk Wood
By Golden Grove 'neath Grongar,
But let me choose and oh! I should
Love all my life and longer
To stroll among our trees and stray
In Goosegog Lane, on Donkey Down,
And hear the Dewi sing all day,
And never, never leave the town.
SECOND VOICE
    The Reverend Jenkins closes the front door. His morning service is over.
    [*Slow bell notes*
FIRST VOICE

Now, woken at last by the out-of-bed-sleepy-head-Polly-put-the-kettle-on townhall bell, Lily Smalls, Mrs Beynon's treasure, comes downstairs from a dream of royalty who all night long went larking with her full of sauce in the Milk Wood dark, and puts the kettle on the primus ring in Mrs Beynon's kitchen, and looks at herself in Mr Beynon's shaving-glass over the sink, and sees:

LILY SMALLS
Oh there's a face!
Where you get that hair from?
Got it from a old tom cat
Give it back then, love.
Oh, there's a perm!
Where you get that nose from, Lily?
Got it from my father, silly.
You've got it on upside down!
Oh, there's a conk!
Look at your complexion!
Oh, no, *you* look.
Needs a bit of make-up.
Needs a veil.
Oh, there's glamour!
Where you get that smile, Lil?
Never you mind, girl.
Nobody loves you.
That's what *you* think.
Who is it loves you?
Shan't tell.
Come on, Lily.
Cross your heart, then?
Cross my heart.
FIRST VOICE

And very softly, her lips almost touching her reflection, she breathes the name and clouds the shaving-glass.

MRS BEYNON (*Loudly, from above*)
Lily!
LILY SMALLS (*Loudly*)
Yes, mum.
MRS BEYNON
Where's my tea, girl?
LILY SMALLS
(*Softly*) Where d'you think? In the cat-box?
(*Loudly*) Coming up, mum.
FIRST VOICE
Mr Pugh, in the School House opposite, takes up the morning tea to Mrs Pugh, and whispers on the stairs
MR PUGH
Here's your arsenic, dear.
And your weedkiller biscuit.
I've throttled your parakeet.
I've spat in the vases.
I've put cheese in the mouseholes.
Here's your . . . [*Door creaks open*
. . . nice tea, dear.
MRS PUGH
Too much sugar.
MR PUGH
You haven't tasted it yet, dear.
MRS PUGH
Too much milk, then. Has Mr Jenkins said his poetry?
MR PUGH
Yes, dear.
MRS PUGH
Then it's time to get up. Give me my glasses.

No, not my *reading* glasses, I want to look *out*. I want to see
SECOND VOICE
Lily Smalls the treasure down on her red knees washing the front step.
MRS PUGH
She's tucked her dress in her bloomers—oh, the baggage!
SECOND VOICE
P.C. Attila Rees, ox-broad, barge-booted, stamping out of Handcuff House in a heavy beef-red huff, black-browed under his damp helmet...
MRS PUGH
He's going to arrest Polly Garter, mark my words.
MR PUGH
What for, dear?
MRS PUGH
For having babies.
SECOND VOICE
... and lumbering down towards the strand to see that the sea is still there.
FIRST VOICE
Mary Ann Sailors, opening her bedroom window above the taproom and calling out to the heavens
MARY ANN SAILORS
I'm eighty-five years three months and a day!
MRS PUGH
I will say this for her, she never makes a mistake.
FIRST VOICE
Organ Morgan at his bedroom window playing chords on the sill to the morning fishwife gulls who, heckling over Donkey Street, observe
DAI BREAD

Me, Dai Bread, hurrying to the bakery, pushing in my shirt-tails, buttoning my waistcoat, ping goes a button, why can't they sew them, no time for breakfast, nothing for breakfast, there's wives for you.

MRS DAI BREAD ONE

Me, Mrs Dai Bread One, capped and shawled and no old corset, nice to be comfy, nice to be nice, clogging on the cobbles to stir up a neighbour. Oh, Mrs Sarah, can you spare a loaf, love? Dai Bread forgot the bread. There's a lovely morning! How's your boils this morning? Isn't that good news now, it's a change to sit down. Ta, Mrs Sarah.

MRS DAI BREAD TWO

Me, Mrs Dai Bread Two, gypsied to kill in a silky scarlet petticoat above my knees, dirty pretty knees, see my body through my petticoat brown as a berry, high-heel shoes with one heel missing, tortoiseshell comb in my bright black slinky hair, nothing else at all but a dab of scent, lolling gaudy at the doorway, tell your fortune in the tea-leaves, scowling at the sunshine, lighting up my pipe.

LORD CUT-GLASS

Me, Lord Cut-Glass, in an old frock-coat belonged to Eli Jenkins and a pair of postman's trousers from Bethesda Jumble, running out of doors to empty slops—mind there, Rover!—and then running in again, tick tock.

BOYO

Me, Nogood Boyo, up to no good in the wash-house.

MISS PRICE

Me, Miss Price, in my pretty print housecoat, deft at the clothes-line, natty as a jenny-wren, then pit-pat back to my egg in its cosy, my crisp toast-fingers, my home-made plum and butterpat.

POLLY GARTER

Me, Polly Garter, under the washing line, giving the breast in the garden to my bonny new baby. Nothing grows in our garden, only washing. And babies. And where's their fathers live, my love? Over the hills and far away. You're looking up at me now. I know what you're thinking, you poor little milky creature. You're thinking, you're no better than you should be, Polly, and that's good enough for me. Oh, isn't life a terrible thing, thank God?

[*Single long high chord on strings*
FIRST VOICE
Now frying-pans spit, kettles and cats purr in the kitchen. The town smells of seaweed and breakfast all the way down from Bay View, where Mrs Ogmore-Pritchard, in smock and turban, big-besomed to engage the dust, picks at her starchless bread and sips lemon-rind tea, to Bottom Cottage, where Mr Waldo, in bowler and bib, gobbles his bubble-and-squeak and kippers and swigs from the saucebottle. Mary Ann Sailors

MARY ANN SAILORS
praises the Lord who made porridge.
FIRST VOICE
Mr Pugh
MR PUGH
remembers ground glass as he juggles his omelet.
FIRST VOICE
Mrs Pugh
MRS PUGH
nags the salt-cellar.
FIRST VOICE
Willy Nilly postman
WILLY NILLY
downs his last bucket of black brackish tea and rumbles out bandy to the clucking back where the hens twitch and grieve for their tea-soaked sops.
FIRST VOICE
Mrs Willy Nilly
MRS WILLY NILLY

full of tea to her double-chinned brim broods and bubbles over her coven of kettles on the hissing hot range always ready to steam open the mail.

FIRST VOICE

The Reverend Eli Jenkins

REVEREND ELI JENKINS

finds a rhyme and dips his pen in his cocoa.

FIRST VOICE

Lord Cut-Glass in his ticking kitchen

LORD CUT-GLASS

scampers from clock to clock, a bunch of clock-keys in one hand, a fish-head in the other.

FIRST VOICE

Captain Cat in his galley.

CAPTAIN CAT

blind and fine-fingered savours his sea-fry.

FIRST VOICE

Mr and Mrs Cherry Owen, in their Donkey Street room that is bedroom, parlour, kitchen, and scullery, sit down to last night's supper of onions boiled in their overcoats and broth of spuds and baconrind and leeks and bones.

MRS CHERRY OWEN

See that smudge on the wall by the picture of Auntie Blossom? That's where you threw the sago.

[*Cherry Owen laughs with delight*

MRS CHERRY OWEN

You only missed me by a inch.

CHERRY OWEN

I always miss Auntie Blossom too.

MRS CHERRY OWEN

Remember last night? In you reeled, my boy, as drunk as a deacon with a big wet bucket and a fish-frail full of stout and you looked at me and you said, 'God has come home!' you said, and then over the bucket you went, sprawling and bawling, and the floor was all flagons and eels.

CHERRY OWEN
Was I wounded?

MRS CHERRY OWEN
And then you took off your trousers and you said, 'Does anybody want a fight!' Oh, you old baboon.

CHERRY OWEN
Give me a kiss.

MRS CHERRY OWEN
And then you sang 'Bread of Heaven,' tenor and bass.

CHERRY OWEN
I *always* sing 'Bread of Heaven.'

MRS CHERRY OWEN
And then you did a little dance on the table.

CHERRY OWEN
I did?

MRS CHERRY OWEN
Drop dead!

CHERRY OWEN
And then what did I do?

MRS CHERRY OWEN
Then you cried like a baby and said you were a poor drunk orphan with nowhere to go but the grave.

CHERRY OWEN
And what did I do next, my dear?

MRS CHERRY OWEN
Then you danced on the table all over again and said you were King Solomon Owen and I was your Mrs Sheba.

CHERRY OWEN (*Softly*)
And then?

MRS CHERRY OWEN

And then I got you into bed and you snored all night like a brewery.
[*Mr and Mrs Cherry Owen laugh delightedly together*
FIRST VOICE
From Beynon Butchers in Coronation Street, the smell of fried liver sidles out with onions on its breath. And listen! In the dark breakfast-room behind the shop, Mr and Mrs Beynon, waited upon by their treasure, enjoy, between bites, their everymorning hullabaloo, and Mrs Beynon slips the gristly bits under the tasselled tablecloth to her fat cat.
[*Cat purrs*
MRS BEYNON
She likes the liver, Ben.
MR BEYNON
She ought to do, Bess. It's her brother's.
MRS BEYNON (*Screaming*)
Oh, d'you hear that, Lily?
LILY SMALLS
Yes, mum.
MRS BEYNON
We're eating pusscat.
LILY SMALLS
Yes, mum.
MRS BEYNON
Oh, you cat-butcher!
MR BEYNON
It was doctored, mind.
MRS BEYNON (*Hysterical*)
What's that got to do with it?
MR BEYNON
Yesterday we had mole.
MRS BEYNON
Oh, Lily, Lily!
MR BEYNON

Monday, otter. Tuesday, shrews.
[*Mrs Beynon screams*
LILY SMALLS
Go on, Mrs Beynon. He's the biggest liar in town.
MRS BEYNON
Don't you dare say that about Mr Beynon.
LILY SMALLS
Everybody knows it, mum.
MRS BEYNON
Mr Beynon never tells a lie. Do you, Ben?
MR BEYNON
No, Bess. And now I am going out after the corgies, with my little cleaver.
MRS BEYNON
Oh, Lily, Lily!
FIRST VOICE
Up the street, in the Sailors Arms, Sinbad Sailors, grandson of Mary Ann Sailors, draws a pint in the sunlit bar. The ship's clock in the bar says half past eleven. Half past eleven is opening time. The hands of the clock have stayed still at half past eleven for fifty years. It is always opening time in the Sailors Arms.
SINBAD
Here's to me, Sinbad.
FIRST VOICE
All over the town, babies and old men are cleaned and put into their broken prams and wheeled on to the sunlit cockled cobbles or out into the backyards under the dancing underclothes, and left. A baby cries.
OLD MAN
I want my pipe and he wants his bottle.
[*School bell rings*
FIRST VOICE

Noses are wiped, heads picked, hair combed, paws scrubbed, ears boxed, and the children shrilled off to school.

SECOND VOICE

Fishermen grumble to their nets. Nogood Boyo goes out in the dinghy *Zanzibar*, ships the oars, drifts slowly in the dab-filled bay, and, lying on his back in the unbaled water, among crabs' legs and tangled lines, looks up at the spring sky.

NOGOOD BOYO (*Softly, lazily*)

I don't know who's up there and I don't care.

FIRST VOICE

He turns his head and looks up at Llareggub Hill, and sees, among green lathered trees, the white houses of the strewn away farms, where farmboys whistle, dogs shout, cows low, but all too far away for him, or you, to hear. And in the town, the shops squeak open. Mr Edwards, in butterfly-collar and straw-hat at the doorway of Manchester House, measures with his eye the dawdlers-by for striped flannel shirts and shrouds and flowery blouses, and bellows to himself in the darkness behind his eye.

MR EDWARDS (*Whispers*)

I love Miss Price.

FIRST VOICE

Syrup is sold in the post-office. A car drives to market, full of fowls and a farmer. Milk-churns stand at Coronation Corner like short silver policemen. And, sitting at the open window of Schooner House, blind Captain Cat hears all the morning of the town.

[*School bell in background. Children's voices.*
The noise of children's feet on the cobbles

CAPTAIN CAT (*Softly, to himself*)

Maggie Richards, Ricky Rhys, Tommy Powell, our Sal, little Gerwain, Billy Swansea with the dog's voice, one of Mr Waldo's, nasty Humphrey, Jackie with the sniff . . . Where's Dicky's Albie? and the boys from Ty-pant? Perhaps they got the rash again.

[*A sudden cry among the children's voices*
CAPTAIN CAT
Somebody's hit Maggie Richards. Two to one it's Billy Swansea. Never trust a boy who barks.
[*A burst of yelping crying*
Right again! It's Billy.
FIRST VOICE
And the children's voices cry away.
[*Postman's rat-a-tat on door, distant*
CAPTAIN CAT (*Softly, to himself*)
That's Willy Nilly knocking at Bay View. Rat-a-tat, very soft. The knocker's got a kid glove on. Who's sent a letter to Mrs Ogmore-Pritchard?
[*Rat-a-tat, distant again*
CAPTAIN CAT
Careful now, she swabs the front glassy. Every step's like a bar of soap. Mind your size twelveses. That old Bessie would beeswax the lawn to make the birds slip.
WILLY NILLY
Morning, Mrs Ogmore-Pritchard.
MRS OGMORE-PRITCHARD
Good morning, postman.
WILLY NILLY
Here's a letter for you with stamped and addressed envelope enclosed, all the way from Builth Wells. A gentleman wants to study birds and can he have accommodation for two weeks and a bath vegetarian.
MRS OGMORE-PRITCHARD
No.
WILLY NILLY (*Persuasively*)
You wouldn't know he was in the house, Mrs Ogmore-Pritchard. He'd be out in the mornings at the bang of dawn with his bag of breadcrumbs and his little telescope . . .

MRS OGMORE-PRITCHARD

And come home at all hours covered with feathers. I don't want persons in my *nice clean* rooms breathing all over the chairs...

WILLY NILLY

Cross my heart, he won't breathe.

MRS OGMORE-PRITCHARD

... and putting their feet on my carpets and sneezing on my china and sleeping in my sheets...

WILLY NILLY

He only wants a *single* bed, Mrs Ogmore-Pritchard.

[*Door slams*

CAPTAIN CAT (*Softly*)

And back she goes to the kitchen to polish the potatoes.

FIRST VOICE

Captain Cat hears Willy Nilly's feet heavy on the distant cobbles.

CAPTAIN CAT

One, two, three, four, five ... That's Mrs Rose Cottage. What's to-day? To-day she gets the letter from her sister in Gorslas. How's the twins' teeth?

He's stopping at School House.

WILLY NILLY

Morning, Mrs Pugh. Mrs Ogmore-Pritchard won't have a gentleman in from Builth Wells because he'll sleep in her sheets, Mrs Rose Cottage's sister in Gorslas's twins have got to have them out...

MRS PUGH

Give me the parcel.

WILLY NILLY

It's for *Mr* Pugh, Mrs Pugh.

MRS PUGH

Never you mind. What's inside it?

WILLY NILLY

A book called *Lives of the Great Poisoners*.

CAPTAIN CAT
That's Manchester House.
WILLY NILLY
Morning, Mr Edwards. Very small news. Mrs Ogmore-Pritchard won't have birds in the house, and Mr Pugh's bought a book now on how to do in Mrs Pugh.
MR EDWARDS
Have you got a letter from *her*?
WILLY NILLY
Miss Price loves you with all her heart. Smelling of lavender to-day. She's down to the last of the elderflower wine but the quince jam's bearing up and she's knitting roses on the doilies. Last week she sold three jars of boiled sweets, pound of humbugs, half a box of jellybabies and six coloured photos of Llareggub. Yours for ever. Then twenty-one X's.
MR EDWARDS
Oh, Willy Nilly, she's a ruby! Here's my letter. Put it into her hands now.
[*Slow feet on cobbles, quicker feet approaching*
CAPTAIN CAT
Mr Waldo hurrying to the Sailors Arms. Pint of stout with a egg in it.
[*Footsteps stop*
(*Softly*) There's a letter for him.
WILLY NILLY
It's another paternity summons, Mr Waldo.
FIRST VOICE
The quick footsteps hurry on along the cobbles and up three steps to the Sailors Arms.
MR WALDO (*Calling out*)
Quick, Sinbad. Pint of stout. And no egg in.
FIRST VOICE
People are moving now up and down the cobbled street.

CAPTAIN CAT
All the women are out this morning, in the sun. You can tell it's Spring. There goes Mrs Cherry, you can tell her by her trotters, off she trots new as a daisy. Who's that talking by the pump? Mrs Floyd and Boyo, talking flatfish. What can you talk about flatfish? That's Mrs Dai Bread One, waltzing up the street like a jelly, every time she shakes it's slap slap slap. Who's that? Mrs Butcher Beynon with her pet black cat, it follows her everywhere, miaow and all. There goes Mrs Twenty-Three, important, the sun gets up and goes down in her dewlap, when she shuts her eyes, it's night. High heels now, in the morning too, Mrs Rose Cottage's eldest Mae, seventeen and never been kissed ho ho, going young and milking under my window to the field with the nannygoats, she reminds me all the way. Can't hear what the women are gabbing round the pump. Same as ever. Who's having a baby, who blacked whose eye, seen Polly Garter giving her belly an airing, there should be a law, seen Mrs Beynon's new mauve jumper, it's her old grey jumper dyed, who's dead, who's dying, there's a lovely day, oh the cost of soapflakes!

[*Organ music, distant*

CAPTAIN CAT
Organ Morgan's at it early. You can *tell* it's Spring.
FIRST VOICE
And he hears the noise of milk-cans.
CAPTAIN CAT
Ocky Milkman on his round. I will say this, his milk's as fresh as the dew. Half dew it is. Snuffle on, Ocky, watering the town ... Somebody's coming. Now the voices round the pump can see somebody coming. Hush, there's a hush! You can tell by the noise of the hush, it's Polly Garter. (*Louder*) Hullo, Polly, who's there?
POLLY GARTER (*Off*)
Me, love.
CAPTAIN CAT

That's Polly Garter. (*Softly*) Hullo, Polly, my love, can you hear the dumb goose-hiss of the wives as they huddle and peck or flounce at a waddle away? Who cuddled you when? Which of their gandering hubbies moaned in Milk Wood for your naughty mothering arms and body like a wardrobe, love? Scrub the floors of the Welfare Hall for the Mothers' Union Social Dance, you're one mother won't wriggle her roly poly bum or pat her fat little buttery feet in that wedding-ringed holy to-night through the waltzing breadwinners snatched from the cosy smoke of the Sailors Arms will grizzle and mope.

[*A cock crows*
CAPTAIN CAT
Too late, cock, too late
SECOND VOICE
for the town's half over with its morning. The morning's busy as bees.

[*Organ music fades into silence*
FIRST VOICE
There's the clip clop of horses on the sunhoneyed cobbles of the humming streets, hammering of horseshoes, gobble quack and cackle, tomtit twitter from the bird-ounced boughs, braying on Donkey Down. Bread is baking, pigs are grunting, chop goes the butcher, milk-churns bell, tills ring, sheep cough, dogs shout, saws sing. Oh, the Spring whinny and morning moo from the clog-dancing farms, the gulls' gab and rabble on the boat-bobbing river and sea and the cockles bubbling in the sand, scamper of sanderlings, curlew cry, crow caw, pigeon coo, clock strike, bull bellow, and the ragged gabble of the beargarden school as the women scratch and babble in Mrs Organ Morgan's general shop where everything is sold: custard, buckets, henna, rat-traps, shrimp-nets, sugar, stamps, confetti, paraffin, hatchets, whistles.

FIRST WOMAN
Mrs Ogmore-Pritchard

SECOND WOMAN
la di da
FIRST WOMAN
got a man in Builth Wells
THIRD WOMAN
and he got a little telescope to look at birds
SECOND WOMAN
Willy Nilly said
THIRD WOMAN
Remember her first husband? He didn't need a telescope
FIRST WOMAN
he looked at them undressing through the keyhole
THIRD WOMAN
and he used to shout Tallyho
SECOND WOMAN
but Mr Ogmore was a proper gentleman
FIRST WOMAN
even though he hanged his collie.
THIRD WOMAN
Seen Mrs Butcher Beynon?
SECOND WOMAN
she said Butcher Beynon put dogs in the mincer
FIRST WOMAN
go on, he's pulling her leg
THIRD WOMAN
now don't you dare tell her that, there's a dear
SECOND WOMAN
or she'll think he's trying to pull it off and eat it.
FOURTH WOMAN
There's a nasty lot live here when you come to think.
FIRST WOMAN
Look at that Nogood Boyo now

SECOND WOMAN
too lazy to wipe his snout
THIRD WOMAN
and going out fishing every day and all he ever brought back was a Mrs Samuels
FIRST WOMAN
been in the water a week.
SECOND WOMAN
And look at Ocky Milkman's wife that nobody's ever seen
FIRST WOMAN
he keeps her in the cupboard with the empties
THIRD WOMAN
and think of Dai Bread with two wives
SECOND WOMAN
one for the daytime one for the night.
FOURTH WOMAN
Men are brutes on the quiet.
THIRD WOMAN
And how's Organ Morgan, Mrs Morgan?
FIRST WOMAN
you look dead beat
SECOND WOMAN
it's organ organ all the time with him
THIRD WOMAN
up every night until midnight playing the organ
MRS ORGAN MORGAN
Oh, I'm a martyr to music.
FIRST VOICE
Outside, the sun springs down on the rough and tumbling town. It runs through the hedges of Goosegog Lane, cuffing the birds to sing. Spring whips green down Cockle Row, and the shells ring out. Llareg-

gub this snip of a morning is wildfruit and warm, the streets, fields, sands and waters springing in the young sun.

SECOND VOICE
Evans the Death presses hard with black gloves on the coffin of his breast in case his heart jumps out.

EVANS THE DEATH (*Harshly*)
Where's your dignity. Lie down.

SECOND VOICE
Spring stirs Gossamer Beynon schoolmistress like a spoon.

GOSSAMER BEYNON (*Tearfully*)
Oh, what can I do? I'll *never* be refined if I twitch.

SECOND VOICE
Spring this strong morning foams in a flame in Jack Black as he cobbles a high-heeled shoe for Mrs Dai Bread Two the gypsy, but he hammers it sternly out.

JACK BLACK (*To a hammer rhythm*)
There is *no leg* belonging to the foot that belongs to this shoe.

SECOND VOICE
The sun and the green breeze ship Captain Cat sea-memory again.

CAPTAIN CAT
No, *I'll* take the mulatto, by God, who's captain here? Parlez-vous jig jig, Madam?

SECOND VOICE
Mary Ann Sailors says very softly to herself as she looks out at Llareggub Hill from the bedroom where she was born

MARY ANN SAILORS (*Loudly*)
It is Spring in Llareggub in the sun in my old age, and this is the Chosen Land.

[*A choir of children's voices suddenly cries out on one, high, glad, long, sighing note*

FIRST VOICE

And in Willy Nilly the Postman's dark and sizzling damp tea-coated misty pygmy kitchen where the spittingcat kettles throb and hop on the range, Mrs Willy Nilly steams open Mr Mog Edwards' letter to Miss Myfanwy Price and reads it aloud to Willy Nilly by the squint of the Spring sun through the one sealed window running with tears, while the drugged, bedraggled hens at the back door whimper and snivel for the lickerish bog-black tea.

MRS WILLY NILLY

From Manchester House, Llareggub. Sole Prop: Mr Mog Edwards (late of Twll), Linendraper, Haberdasher, Master Tailor, Costumier. For West End Negligee, Lingerie, Teagowns, Evening Dress, Trousseaux, Layettes. Also Ready to Wear for All Occasions. Economical Outfitting for Agricultural Employment Our Speciality, Wardrobes Bought. Among Our Satisfied Customers Ministers of Religion and J.P.'s. Fittings by Appointment. Advertising Weekly in the *Twll Bugle*. Beloved Myfanwy Price my Bride in Heaven,

MOG EDWARDS

I love you until Death do us part and then we shall be together for ever and ever. A new parcel of ribbons has come from Carmarthen to-day, all the colours in the rainbow. I wish I could tie a ribbon in your hair a white one but it cannot be. I dreamed last night you were all dripping wet and you sat on my lap as the Reverend Jenkins went down the street. I see you got a mermaid in your lap he said and he lifted his hat. He is a proper Christian. Not like Cherry Owen who said you should have thrown her back he said. Business is very poorly. Polly Garter bought two garters with roses but she never got stockings so what is the use I say. Mr Waldo tried to sell me a woman's nightie outsize he said he found it and we know where. I sold a packet of pins to Tom the Sailors to pick his teeth. If this goes on I shall be in the poorhouse. My heart is in your bosom and yours is in mine. God be with you always Myfanwy Price and keep you lovely for me in His Heavenly Mansion. I must stop now and remain, Your Eternal, Mog Edwards.

MRS WILLY NILLY

And then a little message with a rubber stamp. Shop at Mog's!!!

FIRST VOICE

And Willy Nilly, rumbling, jockeys out again to the three-seated shack called the House of Commons in the back where the hens weep, and sees, in sudden Springshine,

SECOND VOICE

herring gulls heckling down to the harbour where the fishermen spit and prop the morning up and eye the fishy sea smooth to the sea's end as it lulls in blue. Green and gold money, tobacco, tinned salmon, hats with feathers, pots of fish-paste, warmth for the winter-to-be, weave and leap in it rich and slippery in the flash and shapes of fishes through the cold sea-streets. But with blue lazy eyes the fishermen gaze at that milkmaid whispering water with no ruck or ripple as though it blew great guns and serpents and typhooned the town.

FISHERMAN

Too rough for fishing to-day.

SECOND VOICE

And they thank God, and gob at a gull for luck, and moss-slow and silent make their way uphill, from the still still sea, towards the Sailors Arms as the children

[*School bell*

FIRST VOICE

spank and scamper rough and singing out of school into the draggletail yard. And Captain Cat at his window says soft to himself the words of their song.

CAPTAIN CAT (*To the beat of the singing*)

Johnnie Crack and Flossie Snail
Kept their baby in a milking pail
Flossie Snail and Johnnie Crack
One would pull it out and one would put it back
O it's my turn now said Flossie Snail

To take the baby from the milking pail
And it's my turn now said Johnnie Crack
To smack it on the head and put it back
Johnnie Crack and Flossie Snail
Kept their baby in a milking pail
One would put it back and one would pull it out
And all it had to drink was ale and stout
For Johnnie Crack and Flossie Snail
Always used to say that stout and ale
Was *good* for a baby in a milking pail.
[*Long pause*
FIRST VOICE
The music of the spheres is heard distinctly over Milk Wood. It is 'The Rustle of Spring.'
SECOND VOICE
A glee-party sings in Bethesda Graveyard, gay but muffled.
FIRST VOICE
Vegetables make love above the tenors
SECOND VOICE
and dogs bark blue in the face.
FIRST VOICE
Mrs Ogmore-Pritchard belches in a teeny hanky and chases the sunlight with a flywhisk, but even she cannot drive out the Spring: from one of the finger-bowls, a primrose grows.
SECOND VOICE
Mrs Dai Bread One and Mrs Dai Bread Two are sitting outside their house in Donkey Lane, one darkly one plumply blooming in the quick, dewy sun. Mrs Dai Bread Two is looking into a crystal ball which she holds in the lap of her dirty yellow petticoat, hard against her hard dark thighs.
MRS DAI BREAD TWO
Cross my palm with silver. Out of our housekeeping money. Aah!

MRS DAI BREAD ONE
What d'you see, lovie?
MRS DAI BREAD TWO
I see a featherbed. With three pillows on it. And a text above the bed. I can't read what it says, there's great clouds blowing. Now they have blown away. God is Love, the text says.
MRS DAI BREAD ONE (*Delighted*)
That's *our* bed.
MRS DAI BREAD TWO
And now it's vanished. The sun's spinning like a top. Who's this coming out of the sun? It's a hairy little man with big pink lips. He got a wall eye.
MRS DAI BREAD ONE
It's Dai, it's Dai Bread!
MRS DAI BREAD TWO
Ssh! The featherbed's floating back. The little man's taking his boots off. He's pulling his shirt over his head. He's beating his chest with his fists. He's climbing into bed.
MRS DAI BREAD ONE
Go on, go on.
MRS DAI BREAD TWO
There's *two* women in bed. He looks at them both, with his head cocked on one side. He's whistling through his teeth. Now he grips his little arms round one of the women.
MRS DAI BREAD ONE
Which one, which one?
MRS DAI BREAD TWO
I can't see any more. There's great clouds blowing again.
MRS DAI BREAD ONE
Ach, the mean old clouds!
[*Pause. The children's singing fades*
FIRST VOICE

The morning is all singing. The Reverend Eli Jenkins, busy on his morning calls, stops outside the Welfare Hall to hear Polly Garter as she scrubs the floors for the Mothers' Union Dance to-night.

POLLY GARTER (*Singing*)
I loved a man whose name was Tom
He was strong as a bear and two yards long
I loved a man whose name was Dick
He was big as a barrel and three feet thick
And I loved a man whose name was Harry
Six feet tall and sweet as a cherry
But the one I loved best awake or asleep
Was little Willy Wee and he's six feet deep.
O Tom Dick and Harry were three fine men
And I'll never have such loving again
But little Willy Wee who took me on his knee
Little Willy Wee was the man for me.
Now men from every parish round
Run after me and roll me on the ground
But whenever I love another man back
Johnnie from the Hill or Sailing Jack
I always think as they do what they please
Of Tom Dick and Harry who were tall as trees
And most I think when I'm by their side
Of little Willy Wee who downed and died.
O Tom Dick and Harry were three fine men
And I'll never have such loving again
But little Willy Wee who took me on his knee
Little Willy Weazel is the man for me.
REVEREND ELI JENKINS
Praise the Lord! We are a musical nation.
SECOND VOICE

And the Reverend Jenkins hurries on through the town to visit the sick with jelly and poems.

FIRST VOICE

The town's as full as a lovebird's egg.

MR WALDO

There goes the Reverend,

FIRST VOICE

says Mr Waldo at the smoked herring brown window of the unwashed Sailors Arms,

MR WALDO

with his brolly and his odes. Fill 'em up, Sinbad, I'm on the treacle to-day.

SECOND VOICE

The silent fishermen flush down their pints.

SINBAD

Oh, Mr Waldo,

FIRST VOICE

sighs Sinbad Sailors,

SINBAD

I dote on that Gossamer Beynon. She's a lady all over.

FIRST VOICE

And Mr Waldo, who is thinking of a woman soft as Eve and sharp as sciatica to share his bread-pudding bed, answers

MR WALDO

No lady that I know is.

SINBAD

And if only grandma'd die, cross my heart I'd go down on my knees Mr Waldo and I'd say Miss Gossamer I'd say

CHILDREN'S VOICES

When birds do sing hey ding a ding a ding
Sweet lovers love the Spring . . .

SECOND VOICE

Polly Garter sings, still on her knees,
POLLY GARTER
Tom Dick and Harry were three fine men
And I'll never have such
CHILDREN
Ding a ding
POLLY GARTER
again.
FIRST VOICE
And the morning school is over, and Captain Cat at his curtained schooner's porthole open to the Spring sun tides hears the naughty forfeiting children tumble and rhyme on the cobbles.
GIRLS' VOICES
Gwennie call the boys
They make such a noise.
GIRL
Boys boys boys
Come along to me.
GIRLS' VOICES
Boys boys boys
Kiss Gwennie where she says
Or give her a penny.
Go on, Gwennie.
GIRL
Kiss me in Goosegog Lane
Or give me a penny.
What's your name?
FIRST BOY
Billy.
GIRL
Kiss me in Goosegog Lane Billy
Or give me a penny silly.

FIRST BOY
Gwennie Gwennie
I kiss you in Goosegog Lane.
Now I haven't got to give you a penny.
GIRLS' VOICES
Boys boys boys
Kiss Gwennie where she says
Or give her a penny.
Go on, Gwennie.
GIRL
Kiss me on Llareggub Hill
Or give me a penny.
What's your name?
SECOND BOY
Johnnie Cristo.
GIRL
Kiss me on Llareggub Hill Johnnie Cristo
Or give me a penny mister.
SECOND BOY
Gwennie Gwennie
I kiss you on Llareggub Hill.
Now I haven't got to give you a penny.
GIRLS' VOICES
Boys boys boys
Kiss Gwennie where she says
Or give her a penny.
Go on, Gwennie.
GIRL
Kiss me in Milk Wood
Or give me a penny.
What's your name?
THIRD BOY

Dicky.
GIRL
Kiss me in Milk Wood Dicky
Or give me a penny quickly.
THIRD BOY
Gwennie Gwennie
I can't kiss you in Milk Wood.
GIRLS' VOICES
Gwennie ask him why.
GIRL
Why?
THIRD BOY
Because my mother says I mustn't.
GIRLS' VOICES
Cowardy cowardy custard
Give Gwennie a penny.
GIRL
Give me a penny.
THIRD BOY
I haven't got any.
GIRLS' VOICES
Put him in the river
Up to his liver
Quick quick Dirty Dick
Beat him on the bum
With a rhubarb stick.
Aiee!
Hush!
FIRST VOICE
    And the shrill girls giggle and master around him and squeal as they clutch and thrash, and he blubbers away downhill with his patched pants falling, and his tear-splashed blush burns all the way as the tri-

umphant bird-like sisters scream with buttons in their claws and the bully brothers hoot after him his little nickname and his mother's shame and his father's wickedness with the loose wild barefoot women of the hovels of the hills. It all means nothing at all, and, howling for his milky mum, for her cawl and buttermilk and cowbreath and welshcakes and the fat birth-smelling bed and moonlit kitchen of her arms, he'll never forget as he paddles blind home through the weeping end of the world. Then his tormentors tussle and run to the Cockle Street sweet-shop, their pennies sticky as honey, to buy from Miss Myfanwy Price, who is cocky and neat as a puff-bosomed robin and her small round buttocks tight as ticks, gobstoppers big as wens that rainbow as you suck, brandyballs, winegums, hundreds and thousands, liquorice sweet as sick, nougat to tug and ribbon out like another red rubbery tongue, gum to glue in girls' curls, crimson cough-drops to spit blood, ice-cream comets, dandelion-and-burdock, raspberry and cherryade, pop goes the weasel and the wind.

SECOND VOICE

Gossamer Beynon high-heels out of school. The sun hums down through the cotton flowers of her dress into the bell of her heart and buzzes in the honey there and couches and kisses, lazy-loving and boozed, in her red-berried breast. Eyes run from the trees and windows of the street, steaming 'Gossamer,' and strip her to the nipples and the bees. She blazes naked past the Sailors Arms, the only woman on the Dai-Adamed earth. Sinbad Sailors places on her thighs still dewdamp from the first mangrowing cock-crow garden his reverent goat-bearded hands.

GOSSAMER BEYNON
I don't care if he *is* common,
SECOND VOICE
she whispers to her salad-day deep self,
GOSSAMER BEYNON
I want to gobble him up. I don't care if he *does* drop his aitches,

SECOND VOICE
she tells the stripped and mother-of-the-world big-beamed and Eve-hipped spring of her self.
GOSSAMER BEYNON
so long as he's all cucumber and hooves.
SECOND VOICE
Sinbad Sailors watches her go by, demure and proud and schoolmarm in her crisp flower dress and sun-defying hat, with never a look or lilt or wriggle, the butcher's unmelting icemaiden daughter veiled forever from the hungry hug of his eyes.
SINBAD SAILORS
Oh, Gossamer Beynon, why are you so proud?
SECOND VOICE
he grieves to his Guinness,
SINBAD SAILORS
Oh, beautiful beautiful Gossamer B, I wish I wish that you were for me. I wish you were not so educated.
SECOND VOICE
She feels his goatbeard tickle her in the middle of the world like a tuft of wiry fire, and she turns in a terror of delight away from his whips and whiskery conflagration, and sits down in the kitchen to a plate heaped high with chips and the kidneys of lambs.
FIRST VOICE
In the blind-drawn dark dining-room of School House, dusty and echoing as a dining-room in a vault, Mr and Mrs Pugh are silent over cold grey cottage pie. Mr Pugh reads, as he forks the shroud meat in, from *Lives of the Great Poisoners*. He has bound a plain brown-paper cover round the book. Slyly, between slow mouthfuls, he sidespies up at Mrs Pugh, poisons her with his eye, then goes on reading. He underlines certain passages and smiles in secret.
MRS PUGH
Persons with manners do not read at table,

FIRST VOICE

says Mrs Pugh. She swallows a digestive tablet as big as a horse-pill, washing it down with clouded peasoup water.

[*Pause*

MRS PUGH

Some persons were brought up in pigsties.

MR PUGH

Pigs don't read at table, dear.

FIRST VOICE

Bitterly she flicks dust from the broken cruet. It settles on the pie in a thin gnat-rain.

MR PUGH

Pigs can't read, my dear.

MRS PUGH

I know one who can.

FIRST VOICE

Alone in the hissing laboratory of his wishes, Mr Pugh minces among bad vats and jeroboams, tiptoes through spinneys of murdering herbs, agony dancing in his crucibles, and mixes especially for Mrs Pugh a venomous porridge unknown to toxicologists which will scald and viper through her until her ears fall off like figs, her toes grow big and black as balloons, and steam comes screaming out of her navel.

MR PUGH

You know best, dear,

FIRST VOICE

says Mr Pugh, and quick as a flash he ducks her in rat soup.

MRS PUGH

What's that book by your trough, Mr Pugh?

MR PUGH

It's a theological work, my dear. *Lives of the Great Saints.*

FIRST VOICE

Mrs Pugh smiles. An icicle forms in the cold air of the dining vault.

MRS PUGH

I saw you talking to a saint this morning. Saint Polly Garter. She was martyred again last night. Mrs Organ Morgan saw her with Mr Waldo.

MRS ORGAN MORGAN

And when they saw me they pretended they were looking for nests,

SECOND VOICE

said Mrs Organ Morgan to her husband, with her mouth full of fish as a pelican's.

MRS ORGAN MORGAN

But you don't go nesting in long combinations, I said to myself, like Mr Waldo was wearing, and your dress nearly over your head like Polly Garter's. Oh, they didn't fool me.

SECOND VOICE

One big bird gulp, and the flounder's gone. She licks her lips and goes stabbing again.

MRS ORGAN MORGAN

And when you think of all those babies she's got, then all I can say is she'd better give up bird nesting that's all I can say, it isn't the right kind of hobby at all for a woman that can't say No even to midgets. Remember Bob Spit? He wasn't any bigger than a baby and he gave her two. But they're two nice boys, I will say that, Fred Spit and Arthur. Sometimes I like Fred best and sometimes I like Arthur. Who do you like best, Organ?

ORGAN MORGAN

Oh, Bach without any doubt. Bach every time for me.

MRS ORGAN MORGAN

Organ Morgan, you haven't been listening to a word I said. It's organ organ all the time with you . . .

FIRST VOICE

And she bursts into tears, and, in the middle of her salty howling, nimbly spears a small flatfish and pelicans it whole.

ORGAN MORGAN
And then Palestrina,
SECOND VOICE
says Organ Morgan.
FIRST VOICE
Lord Cut-Glass, in his kitchen full of time, squats down alone to a dogdish, marked Fido, of peppery fish-scraps and listens to the voices of his sixty-six clocks—(one for each year of his loony age)—and watches, with love, their black-and-white moony loudlipped faces tocking the earth away: slow clocks, quick clocks, pendulumed heart-knocks, china, alarm, grandfather, cuckoo; clocks shaped like Noah's whirring Ark, clocks that bicker in marble ships, clocks in the wombs of glass women, hourglass chimers, tu-wit-tu-woo clocks, clocks that pluck tunes, Vesuvius clocks all black bells and lava, Niagara clocks that cataract their ticks, old time-weeping clocks with ebony beards, clocks with no hands for ever drumming out time without ever knowing what time it is. His sixty-six singers are all set at different hours. Lord Cut-Glass lives in a house and a life at siege. Any minute or dark day now, the unknown enemy will loot and savage downhill, but they will not catch him napping. Sixty-six different times in his fish-slimy kitchen ping, strike, tick, chime, and tock.

SECOND VOICE
The lust and lilt and lather and emerald breeze and crackle of the bird-praise and body of Spring with its breasts full of riveting May-milk, means, to that lordly fish-head nibbler, nothing but another nearness to the tribes and navies of the Last Black Day who'll sear and pillage down Armageddon Hill to his double-locked rusty-shuttered tick-tock dust-scrabbled shack at the bottom of the town that has fallen head over bells in love.

POLLY GARTER
And I'll never have such loving again,
SECOND VOICE

pretty Polly hums and longs.
POLLY GARTER (*Sings*)
Now when farmers' boys on the first fair day
Come down from the hills to drink and be gay,
Before the sun sinks I'll lie there in their arms
For they're *good* bad boys from the lonely farms,
But I always think as we tumble into bed
Of little Willy Wee who is dead, dead, dead . . . .
[*A silence*
FIRST VOICE

The sunny slow lulling afternoon yawns and moons through the dozy town. The sea lolls, laps and idles in, with fishes sleeping in its lap. The meadows still as Sunday, the shut-eye tasselled bulls, the goat-and-daisy dingles, nap happy and lazy. The dumb duck-ponds snooze. Clouds sag and pillow on Llareggub Hill. Pigs grunt in a wet wallow-bath, and smile as they snort and dream. They dream of the acorned swill of the world, the rooting for pig-fruit, the bag-pipe dugs of the mother sow, the squeal and snuffle of yesses of the women pigs in rut. They mud-bask and snout in the pig-loving sun; their tails curl; they rollick and slobber and snore to deep, smug, after-swill sleep. Donkeys angelically drowse on Donkey Down.

MRS PUGH
Persons with manners,
SECOND VOICE
snaps Mrs cold Pugh
MRS PUGH
do not nod at table.
FIRST VOICE

Mr Pugh cringes awake. He puts on a soft-soaping smile: it is sad and grey under his nicotine-eggyellow weeping walrus Victorian moustache worn thick and long in memory of Doctor Crippen.

MRS PUGH

You should wait until you retire to your sty,
SECOND VOICE
says Mrs Pugh, sweet as a razor. His fawning measly quarter-smile freezes. Sly and silent, he foxes into his chemist's den and there, in a hiss and prussic circle of cauldrons and phials brimful with pox and the Black Death, cooks up a fricassee of deadly nightshade, nicotine, hot frog, cyanide and bat-spit for his needling stalactite hag and bednag of a pokerbacked nutcracker wife.

MR PUGH
I beg your pardon, my dear,
SECOND VOICE
he murmurs with a wheedle.
FIRST VOICE
Captain Cat, at his window thrown wide to the sun and the clippered seas he sailed long ago when his eyes were blue and bright, slumbers and voyages; earringed and rolling, I Love You Rosie Probert tattooed on his belly, he brawls with broken bottles in the fug and babel of the dark dock bars, roves with a herd of short and good time cows in every naughty port and twines and souses with the drowned and blowzy-breasted dead. He weeps as he sleeps and sails.

SECOND VOICE
One voice of all he remembers most dearly as his dream buckets down. Lazy early Rosie with the flaxen thatch, whom he shared with Tom-Fred the donkeyman and many another seaman, clearly and near to him speaks from the bedroom of her dust. In that gulf and haven, fleets by the dozen have anchored for the little heaven of the night; but she speaks to Captain napping Cat alone. Mrs Probert...

ROSIE PROBERT
from Duck Lane, Jack. Quack twice and ask for Rosie.
SECOND VOICE
... is the one love of his sea-life that was sardined with women.
ROSIE PROBERT (*Softly*)

What seas did you see,
Tom Cat, Tom Cat,
In your sailoring days
Long long ago?
What sea beasts were
In the wavery green
When you were my master?
CAPTAIN CAT
I'll tell you the truth.
Seas barking like seals,
Blue seas and green,
Seas covered with eels
And mermen and whales.
ROSIE PROBERT
What seas did you sail
Old whaler when
On the blubbery waves
Between Frisco and Wales
You were my bosun?
CAPTAIN CAT
As true as I'm here
Dear you Tom Cat's tart
You landlubber Rosie
You cosy love
My easy as easy
My true sweetheart,
Seas green as a bean
Seas gliding with swans
In the seal-barking moon.
ROSIE PROBERT
What seas were rocking
My little deck hand

My favourite husband
In your seaboots and hunger
My duck my whaler
My honey my daddy
My pretty sugar sailor
With my name on your belly
When you were a boy
Long long ago?
CAPTAIN CAT
I'll tell you no lies.
The only sea I saw
Was the seesaw sea
With you riding on it.
Lie down, lie easy.
Let me shipwreck in your thighs.
ROSIE PROBERT
Knock twice, Jack,
At the door of my grave
And ask for Rosie.
CAPTAIN CAT
Rosie Probert.
ROSIE PROBERT
Remember her.
She is forgetting.
The earth which filled her mouth
Is vanishing from her.
Remember me.
I have forgotten you.
I am going into the darkness of the darkness for ever.
I have forgotten that I was ever born.
CHILD
Look,

FIRST VOICE
says a child to her mother as they pass by the window of Schooner House,
CHILD
Captain Cat is crying.
FIRST VOICE
Captain Cat is crying
CAPTAIN CAT
Come back, come back,
FIRST VOICE
up the silences and echoes of the passages of the eternal night.
CHILD
He's crying all over his nose,
FIRST VOICE
says the child. Mother and child move on down the street.
CHILD
He's got a nose like strawberries,
FIRST VOICE
the child says; and then she forgets him too. She sees in the still middle of the bluebagged bay Nogood Boyo fishing from the *Zanzibar*.
CHILD
Nogood Boyo gave me three pennies yesterday but I wouldn't,
FIRST VOICE
the child tells her mother.
SECOND VOICE
Boyo catches a whalebone corset. It is all he has caught all day.
NOGOOD BOYO
Bloody funny fish!
SECOND VOICE
Mrs Dai Bread Two gypsies up his mind's slow eye, dressed only in a bangle.
NOGOOD BOYO

She's wearing her nightgown. (*Pleadingly*) Would you like this nice wet corset, Mrs Dai Bread Two?

MRS DAI BREAD TWO

No, I *won't*!

NOGOOD BOYO

And a bite of my little apple?

SECOND VOICE

he offers with no hope.

FIRST VOICE

She shakes her brass nightgown, and he chases her out of his mind; and when he comes gusting back, there in the bloodshot centre of his eye a geisha girl grins and bows in a kimono of ricepaper.

NOGOOD BOYO

I want to be *good* Boyo, but nobody'll let me,

FIRST VOICE

he sighs as she writhes politely. The land fades, the sea flocks silently away; and through the warm white cloud where he lies, silky, tingling, uneasy Eastern music undoes him in a Japanese minute.

SECOND VOICE

The afternoon buzzes like lazy bees round the flowers round Mae Rose Cottage. Nearly asleep in the field of nannygoats who hum and gently butt the sun, she blows love on a puffball.

MAE ROSE COTTAGE (*Lazily*)

He loves me

He loves me not

He loves me

He loves me not

He *loves* me!—the dirty old fool.

SECOND VOICE

Lazy she lies alone in clover and sweet-grass, seventeen and never been sweet in the grass ho ho.

FIRST VOICE

The Reverend Eli Jenkins inky in his cool front parlour or poem-room tells only the truth in his Lifework—the Population, Main Industry, Shipping, History, Topography, Flora and Fauna of the town he worships in—the White Book of Llareggub. Portraits of famous bards and preachers, all fur and wool from the squint to the kneecaps, hang over him heavy as sheep, next to faint lady watercolours of pale green Milk Wood like a lettuce salad dying. His mother, propped against a pot in a palm, with her wedding-ring waist and bust like a black-clothed dining-table, suffers in her stays.

REVEREND ELI JENKINS
Oh, angels be careful there with your knives and forks,
FIRST VOICE
he prays. There is no known likeness of his father Esau, who, undogcollared because of his little weakness, was scythed to the bone one harvest by mistake when sleeping with his weakness in the corn. He lost all ambition and died, with one leg.
REVEREND ELI JENKINS
Poor Dad,
SECOND VOICE
grieves the Reverend Eli,
REVEREND ELI JENKINS
to die of drink and agriculture.
SECOND VOICE
Farmer Watkins in Salt Lake Farm hates his cattle on the hill as he ho's them in to milking.
UTAH WATKINS (*In a fury*)
Damn you, you damned dairies!
SECOND VOICE
A cow kisses him.
UTAH WATKINS
Bite her to death!
SECOND VOICE

he shouts to his deaf dog who smiles and licks his hands.
UTAH WATKINS
Gore him, sit on him, Daisy!
SECOND VOICE
he bawls to the cow who barbed him with her tongue, and she moos gentle words as he raves and dances among his summerbreathed slaves walking delicately to the farm. The coming of the end of the Spring day is already reflected in the lakes of their great eyes. Bessie Bighead greets them by the names she gave them when they were maidens.
BESSIE BIGHEAD
Peg, Meg, Buttercup, Moll,
Fan from the Castle,
Theodosia and Daisy.
SECOND VOICE
They bow their heads.
FIRST VOICE
Look up Bessie Bighead in the White Book of Llareggub and you will find the few haggard rags and the one poor glittering thread of her history laid out in pages there with as much love and care as the lock of hair of a first lost love. Conceived in Milk Wood, born in a barn, wrapped in paper, left on a doorstep, big-headed and bass-voiced she grew in the dark until long-dead Gomer Owen kissed her when she wasn't looking because he was dared. Now in the light she'll work, sing, milk, say the cows' sweet names and sleep until the night sucks out her soul and spits it into the sky. In her life-long love light, holily Bessie milks the fond lake-eyed cows as dusk showers slowly down over byre, sea and town.

Utah Watkins curses through the farmyard on a carthorse.
UTAH WATKINS
Gallop, you bleeding cripple!
FIRST VOICE

and the huge horse neighs softly as though he had given it a lump of sugar.

Now the town is dusk. Each cobble, donkey, goose and gooseberry street is a thoroughfare of dusk; and dusk and ceremonial dust, and night's first darkening snow, and the sleep of birds, drift under and through the live dusk of this place of love. Llareggub is the capital of dusk.

Mrs Ogmore-Pritchard, at the first drop of the dusk-shower, seals all her sea-view doors, draws the germ-free blinds, sits, erect as a dry dream on a high-backed hygienic chair and wills herself to cold, quick sleep. At once, at twice, Mr Ogmore and Mr Pritchard, who all dead day long have been gossiping like ghosts in the woodshed, planning the loveless destruction of their glass widow, reluctantly sigh and sidle into her clean house.

MR PRITCHARD
You first, Mr Ogmore.
MR OGMORE
After you, Mr Pritchard.
MR PRITCHARD
No, no, Mr Ogmore. You widowed her first.
FIRST VOICE
And in through the keyhole, with tears where their eyes once were, they ooze and grumble.
MRS OGMORE-PRITCHARD
Husbands,
FIRST VOICE
she says in her sleep. There is acid love in her voice for one of the two shambling phantoms. Mr Ogmore hopes that it is not for him. So does Mr Pritchard.
MRS OGMORE-PRITCHARD
I love you both.
MR OGMORE (*With terror*)

Oh, Mrs Ogmore.
MR PRITCHARD (*With horror*)
Oh, Mrs Pritchard.
MRS OGMORE-PRITCHARD
Soon it will be time to go to bed. Tell me your tasks in order.
MR OGMORE AND MR PRITCHARD
We must take our pyjamas from the drawer marked pyjamas.
MRS OGMORE-PRITCHARD (*Coldly*)
And then you must take them off.
SECOND VOICE
Down in the dusking town, Mae Rose Cottage, still lying in clover, listens to the nannygoats chew, draws circles of lipstick round her nipples.
MAE ROSE COTTAGE
I'm *fast*. I'm a bad lot. God will strike me dead. I'm seventeen. I'll go to hell,
SECOND VOICE
she tells the goats.
MAE ROSE COTTAGE
You just wait. I'll sin till I blow up!
SECOND VOICE
She lies deep, waiting for the worst to happen; the goats champ and sneer.
FIRST VOICE
And at the doorway of Bethesda House, the Reverend Jenkins recites to Llareggub Hill his sunset poem.
REVEREND ELI JENKINS
Every morning when I wake,
Dear Lord, a little prayer I make,
O please to keep Thy lovely eye
On all poor creatures born to die.
And every evening at sun-down

I ask a blessing on the town,
For whether we last the night or no
I'm sure is always touch-and-go.
We are not wholly bad or good
Who live our lives under Milk Wood,
And Thou, I know, wilt be the first
To see our best side, not our worst.
O let us see another day!
Bless us this night, I pray,
And to the sun we all will bow
And say, good-bye—but just for now!
FIRST VOICE
Jack Black prepares once more to meet his Satan in the Wood. He grinds his night-teeth, closes his eyes, climbs into his religious trousers, their flies sewn up with cobbler's thread, and pads out, torched and bibled, grimly, joyfully, into the already sinning dusk.
JACK BLACK
Off to Gomorrah!
SECOND VOICE
And Lily Smalls is up to Nogood Boyo in the wash-house.
FIRST VOICE
And Cherry Owen, sober as Sunday as he is every day of the week, goes off happy as Saturday to get drunk as a deacon as he does every night.
CHERRY OWEN
I always say she's got two husbands,
FIRST VOICE
says Cherry Owen,
CHERRY OWEN
one drunk and one sober.
FIRST VOICE
And Mrs Cherry simply says

MRS CHERRY OWEN
And aren't I a lucky woman? Because I love them both.
SINBAD
Evening, Cherry.
CHERRY OWEN
Evening, Sinbad.
SINBAD
What'll you have?
CHERRY OWEN
Too much.
SINBAD
The Sailors Arms is always open...
FIRST VOICE
Sinbad suffers to himself, heartbroken,
SINBAD
... oh, Gossamer, open yours!
FIRST VOICE

Dusk is drowned for ever until to-morrow. It is all at once night now. The windy town is a hill of windows, and from the larrupped waves the lights of the lamps in the windows call back the day and the dead that have run away to sea. All over the calling dark, babies and old men are bribed and lullabied to sleep.

FIRST WOMAN'S VOICE
Hushabye, baby, the sandman is coming...
SECOND WOMAN'S VOICE (*Singing*)
Rockabye, grandpa, in the tree top,
When the wind blows the cradle will rock,
When the bough breaks the cradle will fall,
Down will come grandpa, whiskers and all.
FIRST VOICE

Or their daughters cover up the old unwinking men like parrots, and in their little dark in the lit and bustling young kitchen corners, all

night long they watch, beady-eyed, the long night through in case death catches them asleep.
SECOND VOICE
Unmarried girls, alone in their privately bridal bedrooms, powder and curl for the Dance of the World.
[*Accordion music: dim*
They make, in front of their looking-glasses, haughty or come-hithering faces for the young men in the street outside, at the lamplit leaning corners, who wait in the all-at-once wind to wolve and whistle.
[*Accordion music louder, then fading under*
FIRST VOICE
The drinkers in the Sailors Arms drink to the failure of the dance.
A DRINKER
Down with the waltzing and the skipping.
CHERRY OWEN
Dancing isn't natural,
FIRST VOICE
righteously says Cherry Owen who has just downed seventeen pints of flat, warm, thin, Welsh, bitter beer.
SECOND VOICE
A farmer's lantern glimmers, a spark on Llareggub hillside.
[*Accordion music fades into silence*
FIRST VOICE
Llareggub Hill, writes the Reverend Jenkins in his poem-room,
REVEREND ELI JENKINS
Llareggub Hill, that mystic tumulus, the memorial of peoples that dwelt in the region of Llareggub before the Celts left the Land of Summer and where the old wizards made themselves a wife out of flowers.
SECOND VOICE
Mr Waldo, in his corner of the Sailors Arms, sings:
MR WALDO
In Pembroke City when I was young

I lived by the Castle Keep
Sixpence a week was my wages
For working for the chimbley sweep.
Six cold pennies he gave me
Not a farthing more or less
And all the fare I could afford
Was parsnip gin and watercress.
I did not need a knife and fork
Or a bib up to my chin
To dine on a dish of watercress
And a jug of parsnip gin.
Did you ever hear a growing boy
To live so cruel cheap
On grub that has no flesh and bones
And liquor that makes you weep?
Sweep sweep chimbley sweep,
I wept through Pembroke City
Poor and barefoot in the snow
Till a kind young woman took pity.
Poor little chimbley sweep she said
Black as the ace of spades
O nobody's swept my chimbley
Since my husband went his ways.
Come and sweep my chimbley
Come and sweep my chimbley
She sighed to me with a blush
Come and sweep my chimbley
Come and sweep my chimbley
Bring along your chimbley brush!
FIRST VOICE
  Blind Captain Cat climbs into his bunk. Like a cat, he sees in the dark. Through the voyages of his tears, he sails to see the dead.

CAPTAIN CAT
Dancing Williams!
FIRST DROWNED
Still dancing.
CAPTAIN CAT
Jonah Jarvis
THIRD DROWNED
Still.
FIRST DROWNED
Curly Bevan's skull.
ROSIE PROBERT
Rosie, with God. She has forgotten dying.
FIRST VOICE
The dead come out in their Sunday best.
SECOND VOICE
Listen to the night breaking.
FIRST VOICE
Organ Morgan goes to chapel to play the organ. He sees Bach lying on a tombstone.
ORGAN MORGAN
Johann Sebastian!
CHERRY OWEN (*Drunkenly*)
Who?
ORGAN MORGAN
Johann Sebastian mighty Bach. Oh, Bachfach.
CHERRY OWEN
To hell with you,
FIRST VOICE
says Cherry Owen who is resting on the tombstone on his way home.

Mr Mog Edwards and Miss Myfanwy Price happily apart from one another at the top and the sea-end of the town write their everynight letters of love and desire. In the warm White Book of Llareggub you will find the little maps of the islands of their contentment.

MYFANWY PRICE
Oh, my Mog, I am yours for ever.

FIRST VOICE
And she looks around with pleasure at her own neat neverdull room which Mr Mog Edwards will never enter.

MOG EDWARDS
Come to my arms, Myfanwy.

FIRST VOICE
And he hugs his lovely money to his *own* heart.

And Mr Waldo drunk in the dusky wood hugs his lovely Polly Garter under the eyes and rattling tongues of the neighbours and the birds, and he does not care. He smacks his live red lips.

But it is not *his* name that Polly Garter whispers as she lies under the oak and loves him back. Six feet deep that name sings in the cold earth.

POLLY GARTER (*Sings*)
But I always think as we tumble into bed
Of little Willy Wee who is dead, dead, dead.

FIRST VOICE
The thin night darkens. A breeze from the creased water sighs the streets close under Milk waking Wood. The Wood, whose every treefoot's cloven in the black glad sight of the hunters of lovers, that is a God-built garden to Mary Ann Sailors, who knows there is Heaven on earth and the chosen people of His kind fire in Llareggub's land, that is the fairday farmhands' wantoning ignorant chapel of bridesbeds, and, to the Reverend Eli Jenkins, a greenleaved sermon on the innocence of men, the suddenly wind-shaken wood springs awake for the second dark time this one Spring day.

THE END

www.ingramcontent.com/pod-product-compliance
Lightning Source LLC
LaVergne TN
LVHW041928070526
838199LV00051BA/2750